Aspects of Coxwoldshire

A North Yorkshire Local History

Part of Coxwoldshire from the air.

BY

Husthwaite Local History Society

Mrs. I. Ballard, Mr. S. Barker, Mrs. M. Brown, Mr. J. Butler
Mrs. B. Duffield, Dr. S. R. Eyre, Mr. A. Rogers, Mrs. J. Rogers,
Mrs. E. Smith, Dr. D. Wilkinson, Mrs. M. Younger

Editorial Co-ordination David Wilkinson

Published by Husthwaite Local History Society. Copyright 1992
in association with Sessions of York, England

CONTENTS

	Introduction	
1.	Coxwoldshire and its Environment	1
2.	Northumbria and the Conquest	6
3.	The Ancient Landowners	14
4.	Byland Abbey and Newburgh Priory	18
5.	The Civil War and its Aftermath	27
6.	Local Schools in the Nineteenth Century	30
7.	Laurence Sterne, Novelist and Vicar of Coxwold	37
8.	William Peckitt, Glasspainter	40
9.	Agricultural Matters	44
10.	Local News	50
11.	History of a House	54
12.	World War Two	61
13.	Baxby	68
14.	Birdforth	74
15.	Coxwold	77
16.	Newburgh and the Bellasis Family	82
17.	Husthwaite	88
18.	Thornton-on-the-Hill	97
	Index	

ISBN 1 85072 110 6

Typeset by Husthwaite Local History Society

Printed by
William Sessions Limited
The Ebor Press, York, England

Front Cover

Top Left: William Peckitt Top Right: Byland Abbey

Bottom Left: Newburgh Priory Bottom Right: Rev. and Mrs. Winter

INTRODUCTION

Coxwoldshire does not appear on any modern map. Unlike Richmondshire and Hallamshire the name has been lost. The area is, however, still there. It is the valley between the Hambleton and Howardian Hills with the village of Coxwold at its centre. In medieval times the term was frequently used in documents referring to Coxwold, Byland, Newburgh, Husthwaite, Baxby, Thornton-on-the-Hill, Yearsley, Thirkleby and Osgodby. It is possible that the area existed as an administrative unit before the Romans.

In the autumn of 1986 we established a series of lectures through the WEA under the vigorous leadership of Jennifer Kaner. These lasted four years and this book is the result of subsequent work. Our initial aim was to write the history of Husthwaite. It soon became obvious that there were many interesting features beyond Husthwaite's boundaries and we found ourselves drawn into Coxwoldshire.

This account is aimed at the local resident and the interested visitor. It is not an academic work for professional local historians. The chapters are varied in content and reflect the personal interest of the contributors but they are linked by more general work which does give an overall view of the area. It is not comprehensive - such a project was beyond us and would run to several volumes.

ACKNOWLEDGEMENTS

Jennifer Kaner, for her inexhaustible research. The WEA for supporting lecture courses. The Borthwick Institute, University of York, for its helpful tolerance. North Yorkshire County Council Archives Service for access to documents, maps and the Newburgh Papers. Dept. Geography Leeds University for many of the maps. York Art Gallery for William Peckitt illustrations. York City Library. York Minster: Photograph reproduced by kind permission of the Dean and Chapter of York. Photographer: Jim Kershaw. Public Record Office, Kew. Julia Monkman and the Laurence Sterne Trust. Moira Fulton for advising on the Coxwold chapter. Cynthia Wentworth for information on the Slater family. Barry Harrison for his advice on vernacular architecture. Gillian Galloway for reading many of the chapters. Penny Roberts who read and advised on Newburgh. Mr. McDonnell and Rev. J. Macauley OSB, for help on the monasteries. Miss K. Callaway for informing us on the flax factory. Mrs D. Taylor for providing accomodation and allowing us to study the school log book. The Church of the Latter Day Saints, Utah, for access to microfilm of local parish records. The Villagers of Husthwaite for their information and photographs.

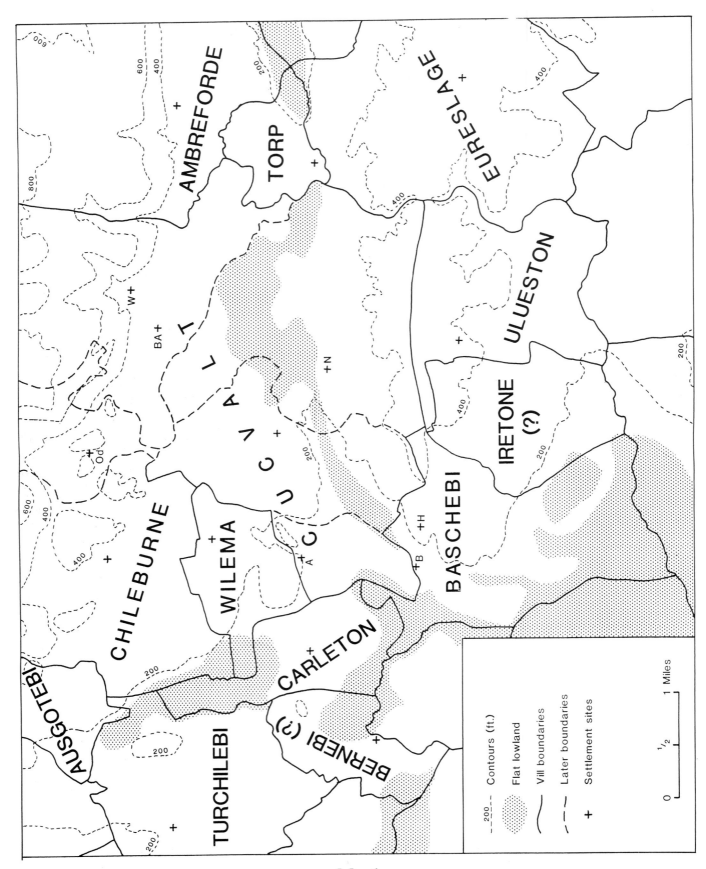

Map 1

Coxwoldshire at the time of Domesday

1
Coxwoldshire and its Environment

S. R. Eyre

"I am as happy as a prince in Coxwold and I wish you could see how princely a manner I live - 'tis a land of plenty which a rich valley under the Hambleton Hills can produce." **Laurence Sterne**

In the heart of North Yorkshire there is a group of attractive and interesting villages. To the north and east they are sheltered from the chilling North Sea winds by the Hambleton and Howardian Hills; on the other side lies the Vale of York and beyond it, on a clear day, the high Pennines around Nidderdale, Wensleydale and Swaledale compose the western horizon. Thirsk is just a few miles away up the A19 and York, in this latter part of the twentieth century, is a mere twenty minutes away to the south. In the past this journey to the Yorkshire metropolis, though doubtless faced with equanimity by those who had to make it, must have been quite an expedition taking more than a single day to accomplish. This book attempts to recapture the appearance of these villages and the activities of the people who have lived in them over the past ten centuries.

Coxwoldshire

To refer to the region covered by these villages and their lands as "Coxwoldshire" is not just a fanciful invention of the twentieth century. The term was clearly in use before medieval times. But whereas old "shire" names like Richmondshire and Hallamshire have survived as regional titles up to modern times, "Coxwoldshire", like many others, fell into disuse. A confirmation of the original twelfth century grant of land by Roger de Mowbray, Lord of Coxwold, for the establishment of Newburgh Priory, refers to the testimony of the twelve elders composing the shire court of Coxwoldshire. It reads: "...*juraverunt duodecim de antiquioribus Cuchewaldi schire...*". [1] A few decades previously the

Domesday Survey itself had shown that this same general area was a unit in terms of ownership and administration. The evidence appears to be quite clear since it indicates that Coxwold (which formerly included both Byland and Newburgh), Baxby (now with Husthwaite), Thornton-on-the-Hill, Yearsley, Thirkleby, Osgodby and part of Ampleforth were all held in one manor by Cofsi, Earl of Northumbria, immediately following the Norman Conquest [MAP 1]. Furthermore, Carlton Husthwaite, the remainder of Baxby (now Husthwaite) and a further portion of Ampleforth, though held by Ulfr at the time of the Conquest, were so intermixed with the lands of Coxwold Manor that they too must formerly have been part of the same unit. To round off the picture, although Angram does not appear in the Domesday record, it is so embedded in the other lands that it was almost certainly part of Coxwold; also the manors of Oulston, Birdforth and Kilburn, though held by other proprietors at the time of Edward the Confessor, are all deeply interlocked with the main manor.

The Geological Setting

Careful analysis of the position on the landscape of this group of villages leads one to suspect that they would never have achieved their administrative unity were it not for a significant geological accident. As the geological map shows [MAP 2] the Jurassic rocks which delineate the eastern edge of the Vale of York dip away eastwards, so that their exposed edges have been eroded into west-facing escarpments which form a fairly abrupt edge to the lowland. This is particularly striking in the Hambleton Hills to the north,

1

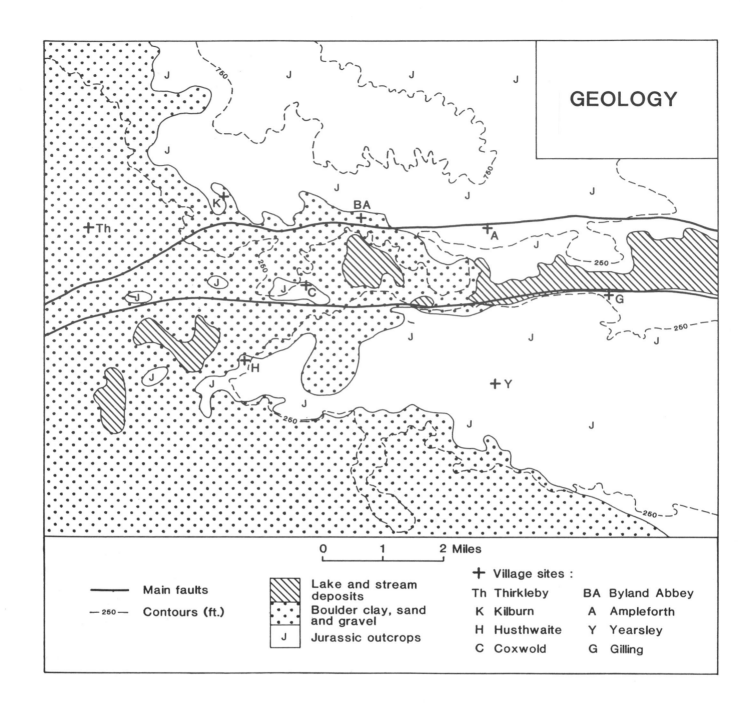

0   1   2 Miles

——— Main faults

— 250 — Contours (ft.)

Lake and stream deposits

Boulder clay, sand and gravel

J   Jurassic outcrops

+ Village sites :

Th Thirkleby   BA Byland Abbey

K   Kilburn   A   Ampleforth

H   Husthwaite   Y   Yearsley

C   Coxwold   G   Gilling

Map 2

where massive sandstones predominate in the strata, but it is still quite pronounced along the western edge of the Howardian Hills where less resistant rocks prevail. There is thus quite an obstacle between the Vale of York and the fertile lowlands of Ryedale and the Carrs lying to the east.

The Coxwold-Gilling Gap

This obstacle would be unbroken were it not for two east-west faults which, millions of years ago, shattered the rocks. The northern one of these runs through Ampleforth and Byland to the south of Kilburn, and the southern one through Gilling and Coxwold. They are known respectively as the Kilburn and Gilling Faults. They came into existence because, under crustal tension, the narrow slice of rock between them, a mere mile and a half in width, dropped down by as much as a thousand feet. This brought down the softer Kimmeridge Clay from the upper Jurassic strata to lie directly against the lower harder Jurassic rocks on either side. Subsequently, over a great period of time, erosion has removed great depths of formerly overlying rock, but considerably more from over the "Coxwold-Gilling Gap" than on either side.

The outcome is that today, a clay vale, referred to by geologists as the "Coxwold-Gilling Gap", runs east-west separating the Hambletons from the Howardians, making it possible to pass from the Vale of York into Ryedale without ever going higher than 225 feet above sea level. So we have a strategic corridor connecting the eastern and central lowlands of what became the North Riding of Yorkshire. In and around this corridor, possibly going far back into prehistory, there developed the estate of Coxwold with its many villages and hamlets. It stretched from Ampleforth in the east, right inside the Coxwold-Gilling Gap, to Baxby, Birdforth and Thirkleby in the west, on the very fringe of the flats and low swells of the Vale of York.

The Ice Age

Another geological episode, much nearer to the present day, has also had a profound effect on settlement and agriculture. Coming between 30,000 and 18,000 BC, long after the bones of the landscape had been established, the last phase of the Pleistocene glaciation impinged upon this bit of territory in a most unusual way. The last ice sheets, coming from the north and north-west, never crossed the highest land of north-east Yorkshire or the land to the south of it. The Cleveland Moors and the fringing hills right down the east coast beyond Scarborough were over-ridden, but the North York Moors, the Hambletons and the Howardians held back the ice so that it never got into the Vale of Pickering [MAP 3]. Since ice blocked the former seaward outlet of the Vale of Pickering just south of Scarborough, all the internal streams and the summer melt water were impounded and the vast body of water which has been traditionally known as "Lake Pickering" was formed. All the evidence indicates that it actually came into contact with the ice front in the Coxwold-Gilling Gap. "Lake Pickering" probably did not survive for very long at its maximum extent; it soon broke through its barriers at the eastern end of the Howardian Hills near Malton and cut a

channel southwards, establishing the present course of the River Derwent in the Kirkham Gorge.

The wider glaciological vista conjures up an intriguing picture of our Coxwoldshire landscape around 18,000 BC, with the ice pushing over the sites of Thirkleby and Carlton Husthwaite right into the enclave where Coxwold, Newburgh and Byland now stand. There the cold waves of this vast glacial lake must have broken against the ice front, while the higher slopes around Oldstead, Oulston and Thornton-on-the-Hill were a treeless land where the sparse tundra vegetation offered little resistance to the frost of winter and the wash of summer melt water. The spur of land upon which Husthwaite now stands was an abrupt obstacle to the ice pushing down the Vale of York from Scotland and the northern Pennines, and this must have pushed uphill here to between 250 and 300 feet above sea level. The great depth of blue Lias clay, scooped up from the Vale, which still plasters some of the Husthwaite hillside, is quite dramatic evidence of the forces which were at work at this time.

The great mass of ice, of course, pushed south-eastward across the Forest of Galtres, coming up against the Howardian slopes all the way, and ultimately reaching the north-western end of the Wolds and becoming spent along the lines of the Escrick and York Moraines at the southern limit of ice encroachment. Even as it died the ice sheet and the resultant meltwater had some significant effects on the landscape. Directly between Husthwaite and Carlton [Maps 4 and 5] there is a flat-bottomed and ill-drained basin appropriately called "Low Ground". The Elphin Beck (headwaters of the Ings Beck) which runs between Husthwaite and Baxby does not flow into or across this depression but goes round it and is separated from it by a string of hummocks of moraine (somewhat mutilated by the making of the railway in 1853-54). But the striking thing is that, at the point of nearest approach, it is actually higher than the surface of the depression by two or three feet. It seems clear that as the ice died a large fragment of it, many acres in extent and many feet thick, was left stranded and half buried in the debris which the ice sheet had brought. The newly formed Elphin Beck, flowing over the surface recently abandoned by the ice, had to flow around this residual

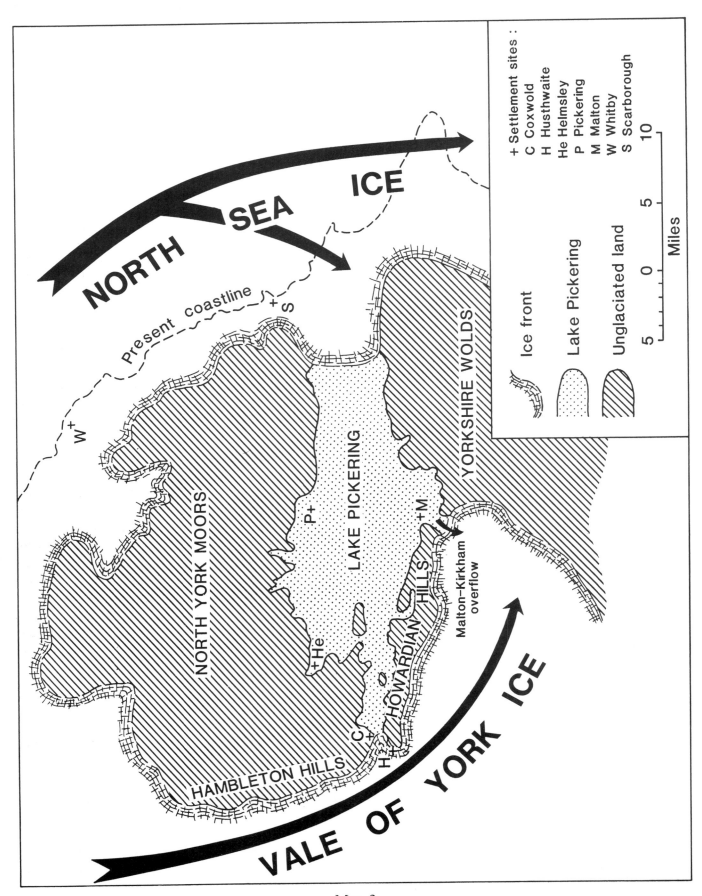

Map 3

The Ice Age

ice fragment cutting down its bed as it did so. When the ice block finally melted it left a "kettle hole" beneath the general level round which the incised stream continued to flow. No doubt this kettle hole carried a small lake for quite a long time until ultimately, it silted up and left this ill-drained hollow, floored with lake deposits.

This is just one of the spectacular sets of deposits which plaster the rocks of this area. They complicate an already complex picture since the underlying Jurassic rocks themselves are very varied. Beds of sandstone, limestone and clay follow one another in rapid succession so that the soils which are formed from them vary from coarse sand to heavy clay and from lime-rich loam to acid peat over very short distances. Add to this that the bed rock may be covered by many feet of sand, gravel or clay which may have been carried great distances by the ice, or washed downslope from areas of quite different rock material, and one can understand why in one small field or even a garden, the soil may vary enormously over just a few square yards.

Soils and Settlement

This is the terrain that farming communities have occupied through the ages, siting their homesteads and selecting the pieces of land which they felt they could cultivate with the greatest profit and the best chance of long term success. Their selection was of fundamental importance because if, even one year in twenty, the crop failed because of drought or waterlogging or flood, then the whole season had been wasted and starvation stared them in the face. We do not know when the first cultivation and permanent settlement took place here, but almost certainly it would be by Neolithic or Bronze Age farmers some thousands of years BC. It could well be that even these early farmers did not have to clear the thick forest which, following the retreat of the ice sheets and the return of warmer conditions, had swathed the landscape of Yorkshire for some thousands of years. No, it could well be that even by 5000 BC, mesolithic hunters had set fire to the forest so that pasture grasses could invade extensively and be an attraction which would cause game animals like deer and wild cattle to congregate more conveniently [2]. This firing would be most effective on drier, better drained slopes rather than on ill-drained flats or lower slopes. Consequently, when peoples of different culture arrived with their flocks, herds and ploughs, they could appropriate the sloping lands with little hindrance. The forest had already been thinned out, and in any case, ill-drained land could not be cultivated on a continuous basis because they did not have the time or techniques to deep-drain the soil, no matter how potentially fertile it might be.

We do not know which sites were first cultivated. Quite a large percentage of the land around all the main settlements in Coxwoldshire is sloping and naturally well-drained, and much of it is both sunny and inherently fertile. Although here and there, Neolithic, Bronze Age and early Iron Age artifacts have been found they do not necessarily indicate the site of a settlement or of cultivated land. The shallow scratchings made by early ploughs have only been detected in a few places in Europe - nowhere in this area - and one can appreciate why this should be so. Such superficial evidence is all too easily removed by subsequent natural development of the soil profile - by frost action and the percolation of rain water; it is certainly obliterated by millennia of subsequent cultivation.

Apart from the occasional burial mound and some miscellaneous earth works whose former function is far from clear, sites of prehistoric human endeavour are not to be found. There is a string of tumuli and earthworks roughly along the line of the ancient routeway known as Malton Street which runs from Aldborough to Brough passing near Husthwaite, Oulston and Yearsley [MAP 1]. But whether archaeology will ever unearth any hard evidence here which will bear witness to the actual location of prehistoric villages and ploughlands remains to be seen.

References

[1] Calendar of Patent Rolls. Vol IV, Nov.2nd, 1389 (13 Richard II): Confirmation by Roger de Mowbray to the Canons and Prior of Newburgh. This document refers to the testimony of the "...twelve elders of Cuchewaldi schire".

[2] Simmons,I.G., "Evidence for vegetation changes associated with mesolithic man in Britain" in P.J. Ucko and J.W. Dimbleby, The Domestication and Exploitation of Plants and Animals, London, 1969, pp 113-22.

2
Northumbria
and the Conquest

S. R. Eyre

It is only for the latter part of the eleventh century, following the Norman Conquest, that there is sufficient evidence to permit an attempt at the overall picture of the patterns of settlement, ownership and cultivation. There is some earlier evidence furnished by place names and a few Anglo Saxon charters, but these apart, we can only speculate about the legacy of Celtic and earlier peoples and the ways in which this was gradually expanded and modified by Anglo Saxon and Danish settlement. It is only with the compilation of Domesday Book [1] in 1086, that we are provided with anything approaching a complete, synoptic account, and even this must be approached with care. It certainly provides evidence for the existence of most of our present day villages and some indication of the ways in which the land appurtenant to each of them was being used. Nevertheless the merest glance at the text of Domesday Book gives clear warning that it requires careful interpretation.

In spite of reservations, however, the point will be sustained below that if the Domesday entries for the North Riding of Yorkshire are viewed in the light of other evidence, not only can a realistic attempt be made to quantify the area of arable land in the years just before 1086, it may even be possible to locate some of the Domesday ploughlands on our present landscape. For some of the villages it certainly seems possible to determine the extent of cultivation with some confidence and precision.

There are three main entries in Domesday Book which refer to this locality: they occur in Folios

327b, 303b and 300d respectively. The first and most substantial one part of the inventory of lands held by Hugh son of Baldric, who was Sheriff of York from 1069 to 1080. The translation[1] is as follows:

(1) "In Coxwold Cofsi had 10c. for g.
In Thornton-on-the-Hill, 3c., Yearsley 3c., Ampleforth 1c., Osgodby 3c., Thirkleby 8c., Baxby 15b. Together 20c. of land less 1b.
There is land for 15p.
Hugh son of Baldric has now there 4p. and 54 villeins having 29p.
In the time of King Edward the Confessor it was worth £6; now (it is worth) £12.
In Kilburn Arnketill had 6c. for g. Land for 3p.
Now Hugh has there 1 villein and 2p.
In Wildon Grange there is soc of this manor of 3c. of land for g. Land for 2p.
11 villeins are there now having 8p.''

The two other excerpts, one regarding lands held by the Archbishop, and the other regarding land held by the King, read as follows:

(2)"In Ampleforth 3c.for g. Ulfr had one manor.
In Baxby, 6c. and 1b. for g. Ulfr had 1 manor.

In Carlton Husthwaite 4 1/2c. for g. Ulfr had 1 manor.''

There follow several other of Ulfr's manors outside Coxwoldshire with lands totaling 6c. 2b. and then:

---

[1]This is a translation from the original latin [1]. The abbreviations used here are as follows: c = carucates (1c = 8 bovates), b = bovate, g = geld and p = ploughs.

6

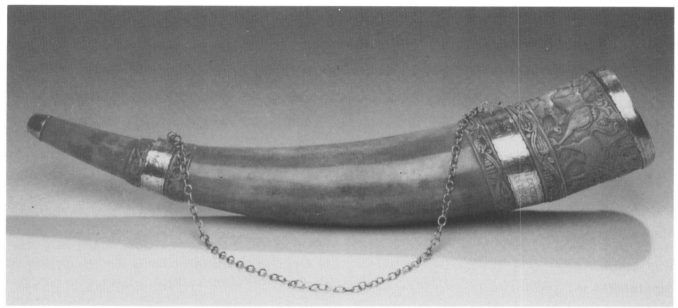

Ulfr's Horn. (Copyright York Minster)

"In all, 19c. and 7b.; and 10p. can be there.
Now St. Peter has them.
They are waste except that 4 villeins having 2p,
render 2/-.
In the time of King Edward they were worth
60/-"

(3) "In Oulston, Gospatric (had) 6c. for g. Land
for 3p.
In Thorpe (Nr.Ampleforth) 3c.for g.. Land for
1p."

A great quantity of information is packed into
these three entries but they are far from self-
explanatory even to those with some understanding of medieval society and economic practices.
However, although there are some persistent
obscurities, these excerpts, along with much of
the rest of Yorkshire Domesday, do have a
certain internal consistency which permits the
formulation of cohesive and persuasive hypoth-
eses.

The Proprietors

There is independent evidence for the existence
and status of some of the proprietors who feature
here. We know Cofsi was a Northumbrian theign
of doubtful reputation who was appointed Earl of
Northumbria by William in 1067, though, in the
eyes of most Northumbrians, Morcar (who had
succeeded Tostig in 1065) was still the rightful
earl, and so remained until the final debacle in
1069. Cofsi was actually slain at Durham a few
months after his appointment. But the really
significant point in the present discussion is that
this strategically situated manor of Coxwold was
clearly part of the estate of the Earl of
Northumbria and could well have been so
traditionally. It is certainly a conspicuous fact
that Cofsi held no other manors within a wide
radius of Coxwold. It seems unlikely to be a
mere accident that this earl's manor was right at
the heart of Birdforth Wapentake - originally
called "Gerlestre Wapentake" (= Earl's Tree)
(see Chapter 13).

The status of the other dramatis personae of
Domesday Coxwoldshire is not so clear, but Ulfr
must have been a freeman of some standing -
almost certainly an important Northumbrian
theign. He held Carlton Husthwaite and large
parts of Baxby and Ampleforth along with many

7

other manors over quite a wide area. His status was such that, sometime between 1066 and 1086, he had been in a position to grant lands to St. Peter (i.e., York Minster). "Ulfr's Horn", mentioned in Camden's History of England, is still held as an important relic in the Treasury of York Minster. Arnketill also must have been a leader of some importance. As well as holding Kilburn and many other manors, he is known from other sources to have been one of the leaders of the Northumbrian rebellion which provoked the savage "Harrying of the North" in 1069.

It is not known what happened to him but there is evidence that Gospatric, the former holder of Oulston, was his son, and that Gospatric was held hostage by the Normans, possibly to discourage any further intransigence by his father.

Population

The Domesday assessment for Coxwold Manor also reveals a very anomalous demographic situation. The overall impression of the condition of northern Yorkshire in 1086 is one of devastation following the "Harrying of the North". An assessment of Domesday population in northern England as a whole indicates that whereas Lincolnshire had nineteen people per square mile, the Vale of York and its surrounding foothills, with a very similar terrain, had only two per square mile [2]. This is well illustrated by some examples in the three extracts which have been quoted. On the Archbishop's lands (extract 2) almost twenty carucates (land for ten ploughs) had been assessed in pre-Conquest times. These had then been worth sixty shillings, but in 1086 they were predominately "waste" with just four villeins using two ploughs and paying two shillings. Many other vills within a ten-mile radius, which had several carucates formerly, were "waste" in 1086. Hutton Sessay and Thormanby which had seven carucates between them were waste. Even those not actually depopulated were nearly all reduced in ploughs and value. Figures such as these, of course, are a mere arid reflection of the conditions of life during the decades following 1069. Few general accounts survive but those that we have paint a dreadful picture of starvation, privation and death, with the wolves increasing and emerging from the woods and hills to prowl undisturbed over the farmland [3]. Fields which had been tilled fell into disuse and any necessity to expand the cultivated area beyond its pre-Conquest limits was obviated for many years to come. The implications of this are discussed later.

In the midst of this picture of disaster and general depopulation it is thus very surprising to encounter an actual increase in population and agricultural potential on Coxwold Manor and at Wildon Grange. We are told that Coxwold had formerly had land for fifteen plough teams and Wildon Grange for two plough teams (seventeen in all), but that in 1086 forty one plough teams (33 + 8) were there. The value of Coxwold had also risen from £6 to £12. In other words there appears to have been a great concentration of people and oxen there, far in excess of those required to till the pre-existing arable land. One is tempted to the hypothesis that Hugh son of Baldric, Sheriff of York until 1080, who now had power of life and death over the whole of this locality (and beyond), had herded together the surviving plough oxen and demoralised peasantry from a wide area so that they could be kept alive and used effectively on his personal estate.

Open Field Agriculture

These Domesday entries may also yield important information about the extent and disposition of cultivated land provided they are viewed cautiously in combination with other evidence. The main entry concerning Coxwold itself can be somewhat confusing particularly in its original unpunctuated latin. When presented in the way in which it appears above, however, its intention seems clear enough. It states quite clearly that in Coxwold itself there were ten carucates for geld. It goes on to say that in the appurtenant vills of Thornton-on-the-Hill, Yearsley, and so on, there were a total of nineteen carucates seven bovates (i.e., twenty carucates of land for geld less one bovate). When punctuated in the way presented clearly this total does not include Coxwold's ten carucates. The total for the whole manor was clearly twenty nine carucates seven bovates and this is the amount of land which is said to be sufficient "for fifteen ploughs", i.e. almost exactly twice as many carucates as ploughs. This 2:1 ratio is repeated in the entries for Kilburn

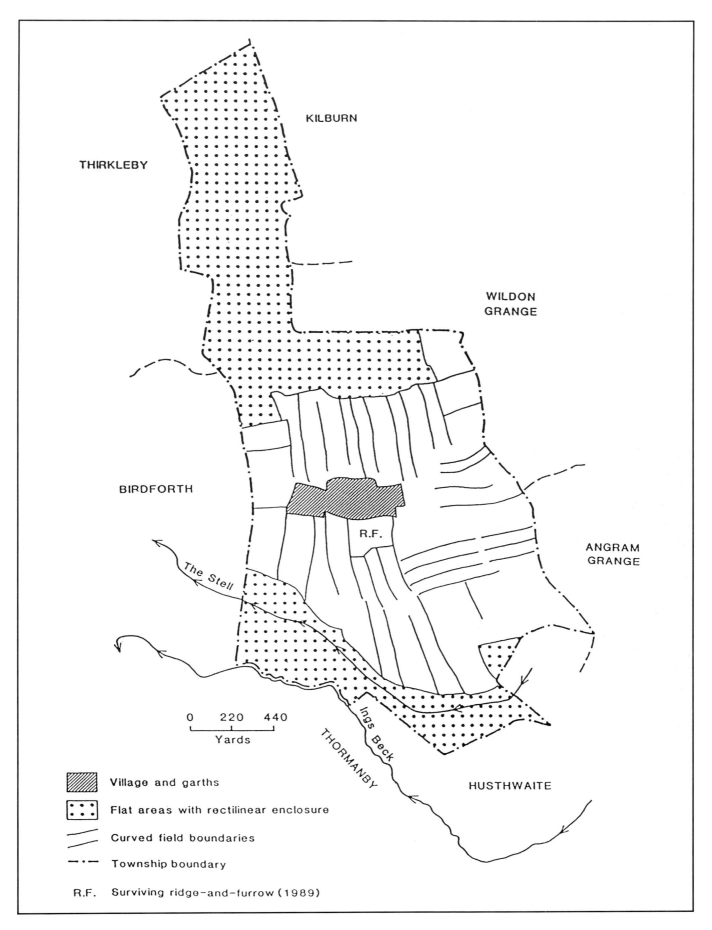

KILBURN

THIRKLEBY

WILDON
GRANGE

BIRDFORTH

R.F.

ANGRAM
GRANGE

The Stell

Ings Beck

THORMANBY

HUSTHWAITE

0   220   440
Yards

▨ Village and garths

⸬ Flat areas with rectilinear enclosure

╱╱ Curved field boundaries

—·—· Township boundary

R.F.   Surviving ridge-and-furrow (1989)

Map 4

Carlton Husthwaite Open Fields

where Arnketill had six carucates for three ploughs, for Oulston where Gospatric also had six carucates for three ploughs, and for the Archbishop's manors where there were nineteen carucates seven bovates for ten ploughs. It is only at Wildon Grange (three carucates to two ploughs) and in Thorpe (3 to 1) that this 2:1 ratio was departed from.

The significance of this kind of information has been disputed by students of Domesday Book for a century or more. It has been held that, by the eleventh century, the "carucate" was a mere taxation device (like the "rateable value" of more recent times) whereby each manor received a statement about the number of units of Danegeld it was liable for and although, undisputably, it was once a true measurement of arable land (the amount that one plough team could manage in a year) it had ceased to be of any value for making even relative statements about the actual amounts of arable land on different manors. This may well be true of other counties but the case is made elsewhere [4] that in the North Riding of Yorkshire if one takes the ratio of geld carucates to ploughteams and considers this in the light of certain aspects of field evidence, some fairly precise inferences may be drawn regarding the location and size of the Domesday ploughlands and the crop rotations practised upon them.

Problems remain but they seem insufficient to invalidate the main conclusions, and pre-eminent among these conclusions is that, in the manors where there is a carucate/plough-team ratio of 2:1, there was a two-field system at the time of the Domesday assessment. Here, in a particular year, half the arable area was in fallow and the other half was under crops; so the number of ploughteams was proportional to the area under crops, but the number of carucates represented the total area available (twice as much).

This is a hypothesis which cannot be proved from documentary evidence - not from Domesday Book itself nor from contemporary documents. We know from later evidence that the two-field system was used in parts of Britain, but direct documentary evidence will probably never show just how extensively. Fortunately there is another strand of evidence which can be used and it is one which is particularly applicable on the

lands of some Coxwoldshire villages. It revolves around the fact that open-field ploughlands over the whole of Western Europe had a characteristic shape: they were laid out in the form of a reversed letter S. Furthermore, wherever these fields were enclosed piecemeal by strip exchange and consolidation, the resultant enclosures had exactly the same form [5]. Many of these fields survived up to the nineteenth century and, by plotting their distribution, it is possible to form a good impression of the location and extent of the open fields.

Carlton Husthwaite

This type of archaeological evidence has survived particularly well in the parishes of Carlton Husthwaite and Husthwaite - parishes which lie on the varied terrain described in Chapter I. It is thus possible to draw maps delineating clearly, first the areas where open-fields existed and, secondly, areas which are so flat and ill-drained that open-field cultivation could never have been contemplated. When this is done for Carlton Husthwaite, with strict objectivity, the whole of its area apart from that covered by the village itself falls into either one category or the other [MAP 4]. The central area around the village is occupied by fields with parallel, curved boundaries, and the significance of this is reinforced by the existence in places of broad ridge-and-furrow with exactly the same reversed-S form. In contrast, to the north lies the flat ill-drained area of Carlton Common, and to the south the "Low Ground" (mentioned in Chapter I) along with the contiguous area along the "Ings Beck". None of this land could be improved until major drainage works such as the Stell had been dug and a proper understanding of the principles of sub-surface drainage was established in the eighteenth and nineteenth centuries.

Since there is no evidence whatever that there have been any material shifts in boundary between Carlton and any of its neighbours it seems that we have here a Domesday manor where the maximum extent of open field cultivation can be determined with some precision. Domesday Book states that it had 4.5 carucates and that it was part of the Archbishop's lands which totalled nineteen carucates seven bovates and where there was land for ten ploughs [extract

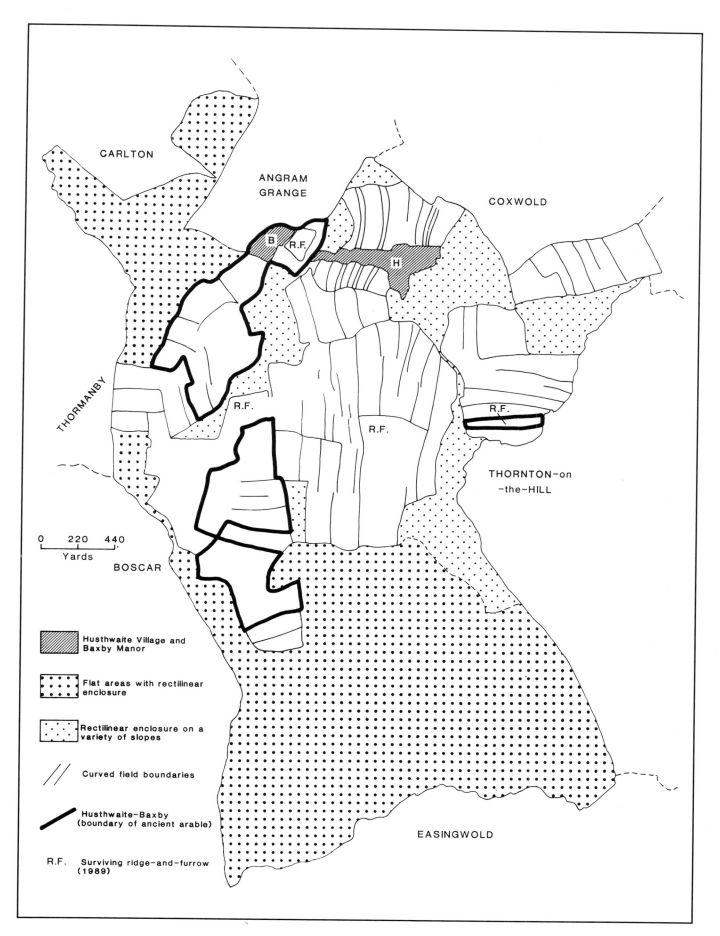

CARLTON

ANGRAM
GRANGE

COXWOLD

B R.F.

H

THORMANBY

R.F.

R.F.

R.F.

THORNTON-on
-the-HILL

0   220   440
Yards

BOSCAR

Husthwaite Village and
Baxby Manor

Flat areas with rectilinear
enclosure

Rectilinear enclosure on a
variety of slopes

Curved field boundaries

Husthwaite-Baxby
(boundary of ancient arable)

EASINGWOLD

R.F.   Surviving ridge-and-furrow
(1989)

Map 5

Husthwaite Open Fields

11

2]. On the basis of the premises arrived at above one thus deduces that it had a two-field system.

Also significant is that when the former open field in Carlton is measured on the map, one arrives at an area of 430.4 acres (174.2 ha.). In other words, if this open field area is the 4.5 carucates recorded in Domesday Book then the carucate in Carlton averaged just under ninty six acres (i.e., the bovate size was just under twelve acres). It can be objected that we have no proof that the area measured here is the area assessed for geld in pre-Conquest times: is it not possible that the area of open field either expanded or contracted materially in the following centuries? There are good reasons for doubting this. First, as just demonstrated, there can be no question of the open field area ever having been any larger: the nature of the terrain did not allow it. Secondly it seems unlikely that there would be an expansion of the open field agriculture (from a smaller area in 1086) during the following two centuries because of the greatly reduced population. As noted above it must have taken some generations before the pre-Conquest population pressure was re-established. Furthermore the change from a two-field to a three-field system which may have taken place would also have decreased the tendency to expansion of the open field area. A ninety six-acre carucate would have only forty eight acres bearing crops in any one year, but if there were a change to a three-field system then sixty four acres would be in cultivation - an increase of sixteen acres. If this kind of change was brought about, say, over all the twenty carucates held by the Archbishop, then this would entail an extra 320 acres of crops per annum with no actual expansion of the open field. So if twelve acres of crops could support one family, then an increase of 320 acres represents crops for more than twenty five families. Thirdly, if anyone wishes to sustain the argument that in Carlton Husthwaite the Domesday open field area was significantly smaller than that ultimately achieved, then they are arguing for a carucate materially less than ninety six acres i.e., a bovate of less than twelve acres. This would not be in accordance with all kinds of independent evidence for the north of England.

Husthwaite and Baxby

Husthwaite is the one large village of Coxwold-shire which receives no mention (as such) in Domesday Book. However, it will not have escaped notice that Baxby has two entries showing that the Lord of Coxwold held a manor of one carucate seven bovates, and that Ulfr held another (now granted to the Archbishop) of six carucates one bovate. It will be demonstrated here that this second holding (the larger of the two) was almost certainly Husthwaite, though there is no documentary evidence for this name until 1167 when it was noted (along with Oulston and Thornton) as one of the manors just outside the boundaries of the Royal Forest of Galtres [Pipe Rolls,1167]. We do know for certain that it had a "chapel" by 1154 because a document of Newburgh notes retrospectively that by an agreement between St. Peter's and Newburgh, a monk of Newburgh called "Brian" had been appointed as priest some time between 1145 and 1154.

The name "Husthwaite" may well have a deeper significance. Historical geographical research is showing increasingly that quite a number of the our northern civil parishes may have begun, not as single village nucleations with large open fields concentrated around them from which daughter settlements (outlying farms and hamlets) all sprang at a later stage, but, conversely, as a scattering of almost equally ancient clearings in the forest which were later consolidated into single manorial units. It could be that Baxby in Anglo-Saxon and Danish times, grew to be a sizeable manor in this way, with separate clearings (or "thwaites") around Baxby, Husthwaite, Acaster Hill, Woolpots and Highthorne. If one of these thwaites developed fastest and had the largest group of houses on it (and ultimately the consecrated church), what is more likely than that this became referred to as the "hus - thwaite". It might even be that it developed this special connotation because this was the "thwaite" where, because of population expansion in the pre-Conquest days, the dwellings and their appurtenant crofts or garths were already starting to encroach on already established open-field strips. This is a scenario which must not be regarded as anything but hypothetical, but there is much in the documents and the landscape to support it. It will be noted, for instance (MAP 5), that the garths behind the village tenements along the main street have a curvature which indicates that they began their existence as strips in the open fields.

The view that the two Domesday Manors of Baxby are the same as the present day Baxby and Husthwaite seems inescapable because right up to the nineteenth century there were two townships with these names which were separate but, nevertheless, intimately connected with each other. In fact Baxby township lay in seven separate parcels, each one partly or completely embedded in Husthwaite [MAP 5]. What clearer evidence could one have that the two were formerly one manor? And can there be any doubt that this division took place before 1066, at a date when Ulfr, or one of his predecessors, and the Lord of Coxwold divided it between them?

All this bears witness to the enormous stability of township boundaries in this area, and is illustrated in a most startling way by one particular locality. Over on the eastern side of this jointly held area (beside what is now Sand Hill Farm) is a curved strip of land approximately 6.5 acres in extent. This is shown as part of Baxby township on both the Tithe Survey and the 1st edition of the Ordnance Survey, though it is completely surrounded by Husthwaite [MAP 5]. Nothing could more clearly substantiate the view that Baxby (Coxwold) and Baxby (Ulfr) were formerly one, so that when the division took place a half bovate of one was left stranded in the other.

It is possible to analyze the whole area of Husthwaite (1677 acres) and Baxby (333 acres) in the same way as for Carlton, though the operation at some points is more problematical. This is mainly because, as well as the flat ill-drained land, these two townships had some steeper areas on which there is no field evidence for former open-field usage. Over a small fraction of the area there is thus a little more room for doubt: very steep areas are certainly unlikely to have been under open-field usage, but one cannot be so confident about this as one can with ill-drained morass. However, the main picture is clear and the boundaries have been drawn objectively, just as with Carlton. On the basis of this, 607.9 acres of Husthwaite and 194.13 acres of Baxby are diagnosed as former open field. If this was essentially the land assessed in the Domesday carucates, the forty nine bovates (six and one eighth carucates) of Husthwaite must have averaged 12.40 acres and those of Baxby (fifteen bovates) 12.96 acres. These average bovate sizes are not far removed from that of 11.96 for Carlton.

The System

So the field evidence for Carlton, Baxby and Husthwaite, when viewed alongside the Domesday record, seems to provide the basis for a coherent hypothesis regarding the extent of the open fields prior to the Conquest, and the rotations practised within them. It seems reasonable to envisage most of the Coxwoldshire townships as having carucates of around a hundred acres each, managed in two-field systems. In the main each pair of carucates would thus be managed by one plough team and each team would plough half a carucate before Christmas and the other half afterwards. On the other hand, townships like Wildon Grange would have three carucates managed by two plough teams in three-field systems. Evidence for the whole of the North Riding does seem to support this view of things [4].

Research into historical obscurities like those explored here only seems to have a chance of success with townships like Carlton and Husthwaite where the terrain and the field and map evidence provide windows through which the obscure interior of the scriptorium can be examined.

References

[1] Adapted from the translation by Margaret L. Faull and Marie Stimson (eds.) in Domesday Book, John Morris (Gen.ed.), Vol.30 "Yorkshire", Parts 1 and 2, 1986.

[2] H.C. Darby and I.S.Maxwell., The Domesday Population of Northern England, 1962, Fig.30, p.121.

[3] Marjorie Chibnall, The Ecclesiastical History of Orderic Vitalis, Vol.2, 1969-75.

[4] S.R.Eyre, "Open-field cultivation and the Domesday record for the North Riding of Yorkshire", Working Paper, School of Geography, University of Leeds, No. 91/7, 1991.

[5] S.R.Eyre, "The curving plough-strip and its historical implications", Agric. Hist. Rev. IV, 1955, pp.80-94

3

The Ancient Landowners

For many centuries most of Coxwoldshire and the land surrounding Thirsk was owned by the Mowbray family - the northern part of the Vale of York, the Vale of Mowbray, still bears their name. The family which came over with William the Conqueror from Montbray, now only a small village on the river Drom near St. Lo, in Normandy, was to become one of the most famous families in English history. For over four hundred years, until the line was lost with the death of Ann de Mowbray in 1481, they grew in influence, acquiring the titles Earl of Nottingham, Earl Marshal and Duke of Norfolk.

Before the conquest most of Coxwoldshire was owned by **Cofsi**, who had probably got it from Tostig, King Harold's brother (see Chapter 2). After Cofsi's death the lands passed to **Hugh Son of Baldric**, a wealthy Norman who was Sheriff of York. Unfortunately he supported Robert, William's brother, in his attempts to take the throne and forfeited his lands in about 1089.

Robert de Stuteville was then given the area and held it until 1106 when at the Battle of Tinchebrai he supported Robert of Normandy against Henry I. This battle was decisive for Henry to rule in both England and France. De Stuteville had to forfeit his possessions to **Nigel d'Aubigny** the founder of the second House of Mowbray. Although the Stutevilles were to dispute the Mowbrays' claim in coming generations the ownership of most of Coxwoldshire was set for the next four hundred years.

Husthwaite did not become part of the Mowbray fee as it had been given to the Archbishop of York by **Ulfr** before 1086 and was to remain church property until the nineteenth century with a canon of the Minster acting as lord of the manor or prebend.

The Mowbrays

The first Mowbray in England was **Roger de Montbray** who was succeeded by **Robert de Mowbray**, Earl of Northumbria who died in 1125.

MOWBRAY. Gules a lion argent.

Robert was described as rich, bold, fierce, haughty, a despiser of equals, swollen with vanity, of great stature, strong and hairy. He had a powerful uncle in Geoffrey, Bishop of Countances and a follower of the Conqueror. They sided with Robert against William Rufus and burnt Bath, sacking much of the West Country...but when the revolt collapsed the king did not feel strong enough to punish them. Later Robert was to slay King Malcolm of the Scots at Alnwick. On his uncle's death Robert succeeded to all his wealth including 280 manors.

At this point he became over-confident and tried to take the crown for his cousin, Stephen of Humale, but was defeated at Banburgh and imprisoned for life, ending the first house of Mowbray. Shortly before his imprisonment he had married **Matilda** but the Pope admitting she was a widow in all but name allowed her to remarry Nigel d'Aubigny. This marriage was probably sanctioned by Henry I to give Nigel status and land. He was a ''new man'' who as a younger son had not inherited from his Norman family. He had gained Henry's support at the Battle of Tinchebrai and between 1107 and 1118 was deeply involved in the government of the

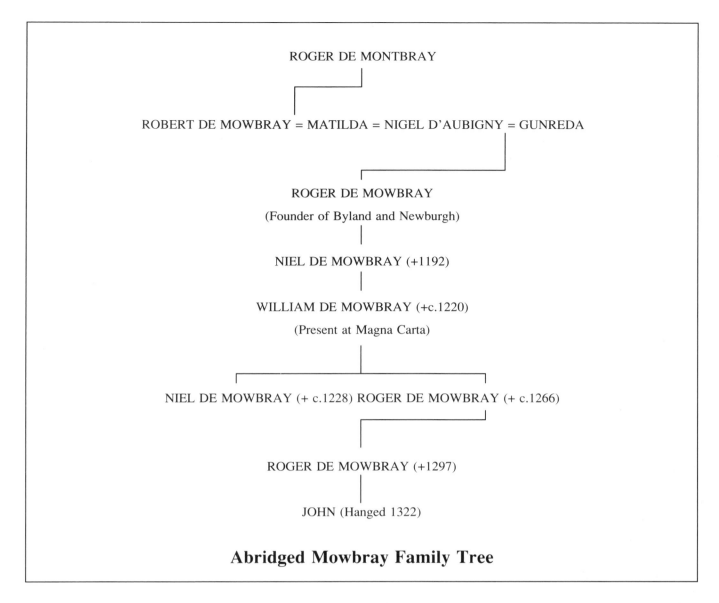

ROGER DE MONTBRAY

ROBERT DE MOWBRAY = MATILDA = NIGEL D'AUBIGNY = GUNREDA

ROGER DE MOWBRAY

(Founder of Byland and Newburgh)

NIEL DE MOWBRAY (+1192)

WILLIAM DE MOWBRAY (+c.1220)

(Present at Magna Carta)

NIEL DE MOWBRAY (+ c.1228)   ROGER DE MOWBRAY (+ c.1266)

ROGER DE MOWBRAY (+1297)

JOHN (Hanged 1322)

Abridged Mowbray Family Tree

North and was frequently at the king's side. Henry gave him a large number of manors to form the ''Honour of Mowbray'' which was complete by 1115, much of it derived from the estates which William Rufus had given to the Stutevilles.

His son, **Roger de Mowbray**, by a second marriage to **Gunreda**, was to be one of the most influential individuals shaping Coxwoldshire. He was, however, not as powerful as his father and did not enjoy royal protection, making his defence of the Honour often difficult. At times Roger lived at Thirsk and from there founded the abbeys of Byland and Newburgh. As a young man he was present at the Battle of the Standard at Northallerton and a few years later was captured at the Battle of Lincoln by Ranulf, Earl of Chester. On his return from the second crusade Roger tried to take York and in local skirmishes, Myton Bridge was destroyed and

Ripon damaged. He supported the rebellion against Henry II in 1174 and with Stuteville help was deprived of his castles at Thirsk and Kirkby Misperton. He fled to Scotland but had them restored in 1177. After this he moved his main residence to Epworth in Axholme. On another crusade to the Holy Land he was captured by the Saracens at the Battle of Hittin and died soon after his ransom in 1188. Some accounts say he died at Tyre and others that he returned to live at Hood Castle with a lion; this was probably an elaboration of the monks. He was thought to have been buried at Byland Abbey and in 1819 the Stapylton family removed a body to their estate at Myton. It was later returned and probably the bones were those of an abbot.

Succeeding generations of Mowbrays were to be prominent in English history. William, Roger's grandson, was one of the barons who forced King John to sign Magna Carta in 1215. John,

Lord Mowbray (born 1286) was distinguished in the wars with Scotland and knighted before his majority but was to fall into disfavour and join the insurrection of the Earl of Lancaster. He was taken prisoner at the Battle of Boroughbridge and hanged at York in 1322. Thomas, 1st Duke of Norfolk, was closely associated with Richard II; his quarrel with Henry Bolingbroke, later to be Henry IV, was the subject of Shakespeare's first act of Richard II. It resulted in Thomas being banished to Italy where he died in 1400. The last Mowbray was Anne who married Richard, one of the "Princes of the Tower"; she died shortly after her husband and the Mowbray line was extinguished.

The Honour of Mowbray

There were six main Lordships to the Honour of Mowbray created by Henry I for Nigel d'Aubigny; in Leicestershire around Melton, Warwickshire, the Isle of Axholme in Lincolnshire, Burton Lonsdale and Thirsk. At its peak it was worth 100 knights' fees and was one of the greatest fiefs in England. This was to be the power base for succeeding Mowbrays.

Not all the manors were held for the Mowbrays' own use as Demesne estates but many were let to household knights in return for military services. Also, as we have seen, some land was given to religious houses and small holdings passed to servants lower in the social scale, such as archers and millers.

The demesne estates all had castles or manors and fed the lord and his household, who would move around them during the year - some said when the stench in one grew too much. On Nigel's death in 1129 he had thirteen of his most valuable manors held in demesne though this was down to seven by 1170. The largest was at Axholme with Thirsk second.

The Honour was administered by a military chief, the constable; the steward who managed the tenants; a chamberlain as finance officer and a chaplain. The Honour held a series of courts which transacted property transfers and arbitrated in disputes between tenants.

Most of the ancient manors of Coxwoldshire were tenanted by knights of the Mowbray family.

The Daivilles (d'ayville and d'eyvill) are thought to be descended from the Mowbrays and a Robert Daiville was constable to Robert Mowbray in 1184. He held

DAIVILLE. Or a esse gules with six fleurs de lis over all counter-coloured

Thornton-on-the- Hill, Baxby and Kilburn together with estates in Leicestershire and Nottinghamshire. They do not appear to have been involved in the rebellion against King John but they supported Simon de Montfort against Henry III. During this uprising the barons entered York and sacked St. Mary's Abbey. Because John Daiville borrowed money from the Jews, possibly to "square" his account with the crown, a good description of Thornton exists for this period.

The Daivilles at this time made a gift of part of Kilburn to Byland Abbey and by the fourteenth century the whole had passed into Byland's hands.

They regained Thornton in 1276 by an arrangement with one of the creditors, Fetler Byset, who was known as "Le Taburner", to whom they paid 578 marks. Before 1307 they leased Thornton to Isabel de Vesci and the ownership of the manor after that date is complicated. It was eventually taken over by the Bellasis family in 1608 and much of it is still owned by the Newburgh Estate.

The Baxby manor was probably held by the Daivilles and their descendants until the seventeenth century when it too passed to the Bellasis family. In the sixteenth century it was held by the Baxby family as subtenants of the Daivilles and later by John Chambers who married a Baxby.

The Maunsells of Birdforth were subtenants of the **Malbisses** - a Hugh Malbisse was a steward of the Mowbrays in the twelfth century. The Malbisses were involved in 1190 when jews were

MAUNSELL. Or a fesse dancetty gules with three lions argent thereon.

COLVILLE. Argent a cross paty gules.

attacked in York and derived the name of "Mal-beasts". The family was in the group of northern barons who forced King John to sign the Magna Carta and a Richard Malbisse is recorded as using oaks to build a castle at Wheldrake. Part of the manor of Birdforth passed into the Honour of Eye and by the sixteenth century was held by the Earl of Leicester and it followed the descent of Raskelf manor. Another part of the manor was sold to Sir Thomas Dawney in 1605 and passed into Lord Downe's estate.

The **Colville** family were military subtenants of the Mowbrays and Thomas Colville was enfeoffed by Roger de Mowbray in the manors of Coxwold, Yearsley and Oulston before 1166. The Colvilles probably held Coxwold until 1590 when it passed to the Bellasises. Colville Hall still stands near to the church and next to Manor Farm to which it may have been joined. Most of the land owned in Oulston was granted to Newburgh Priory.

Sources

[1] Greenway D.E., Mowbray Charters. 1972.
[2] Dictionary of National Biography
[3] In Well Beware. Smith G.R.
[4] Victoria County History. North Yorkshire.

View across Coxwoldshire from the Beacon to the Hambleton Hills and the White Horse

4
Byland Abbey and Newburgh Priory

Mary Brown

BYLAND ABBEY

The stones of the Cistercian abbey at Byland still speak to us of a religious house described eight centuries ago, by William of Newburgh, as one of the three luminaries of the north. The companions were the abbeys of Fountains and Rievaulx. What we see now are the remains, dominated by the impressive west front of the church. The most striking feature is the semi-circular curve of what was a magnificent rose window, twenty six feet in diameter, flanked by a finely shaped turret pointing heavenwards.

Origins

For centuries monks throughout Europe followed the Rule of St. Benedict, first promulgated in the seventh century. In the middle years of the eleventh century small numbers of men felt the need to lead a simpler, stricter form of monastic life. In northern France one of the first was a group at Savigny led by Vitalis of Mortain and from whence came the monastic company at Furness in Cumbria. Further to the south in the woodlands of Burgundy a group of hermits sought a desolate place and thought to offer their lives in poverty, prayer and seclusion. Their first abbot was Robert of Molesme but the company transferred to the forest of Citeaux, which gave its name, Cistercian, to the order. The outstanding characters emerging were Stephen Harding, an Englishman and Bernard of Clairvaux.

The Cistercian way of life was austere, a life of prayer, study of the scriptures, of silence and an essential element - manual labour. Physically remote from society, they did not associate themselves with parish churches, accept tithes or any material wealth other than the land which was to be their support. It was from Clairvaux that monks came in 1131 to settle on the banks of the Rye and begin the illustrious house of

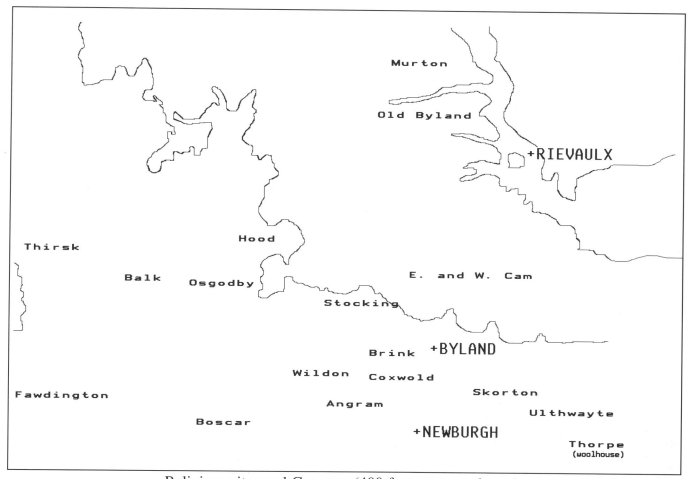

Religious sites and Granges. (400 foot contour shown).

Rievaulx.

Foundation at Hood

In the same spirit of poverty a band of twelve monks, led by Abbot Gerold, had left the Savigniac Abbey of Furness to settle in Calder. Three years later, in 1137, they were driven out by raiding Scots and being refused readmission at Furness they set off on a long journey to York, seeking the help of Archbishop Thurston. Their means of transport was a wagon drawn by a team of eight oxen. Their only worldly wealth was their clothes, the grey habit of Savigny, and the necessary books of the liturgy. On reaching Thirsk they were given shelter by Gunreda, mother of Roger de Mowbray. For the next four years they lived at Hood at the foot of Sutton Bank where a monk, Robert d'Alney, Gundreda's uncle from Whitby, was already living as a hermit. Even at this early stage Roger de Mowbray was making grants of lands to the monks. In 1140 he gave them land between the fields of Coxwold and Kilburn, his cattle station

at Cambe and the whole townships of Great Wildon and Little Wildon. This was important as the first of Byland's granges. Among its early occupants were three of de Mowbray's knights who, having fought with him at Northallerton at the Battle of the Standard, were admitted to the community as lay brothers.

Moves to Old Byland and Stocking

Abbot Gerold died in 1142 and was buried at Hood. He was succeeded by Roger who held the office of abbot for fifty-four years. In 1143, when the site at Hood could no longer hold their numbers, the monks appealed to de Mowbray who gave them land at Old Byland near the river Rye. It proved to be too close to Rievaulx Abbey, the bells of each abbey being heard by the monks of the other. Four years later their benefactor gave them two carucates (c. 240 acres) at Stocking, probably where Oldstead Hall is now. There according to Abbot Philip, writing in 1197, "they built a small stone church, a cloister and other houses and workshops". This move coincided with an application from the Savignac Order to be absorbed into the order of Cistercians - a change that was made permanent in the following year.

De Mowbray continued to endow the monks with land, in Coxwold, Bagby, Balk, Hovingham, Yearsley and as far away as Nidderdale. Sometimes the grant was first made by one of his knights, who held lands within his estates. An example of this is the whole territory of Thorpe, near Ampleforth, which William de Wydevilla gave to the monks. It was confirmed by Roger and is recorded in the Charters of the Honour of Mowbray. Thomas de Colville held Coxwold and made substantial gifts including the escarpment east of Wass, land between Brink Hill and Long Beck, twenty acres in the wood between Thorpe and Yearsley and the road between the abbey and Wildon.

BYLAND ABBEY

Gules a lion argent with

a crosier or bend sinister -

wise athwart him.

The name Daiville (sometimes d'eyvil, Davidville, Dayville, or Dayvil) of Kilburn occurs frequently in Byland's history and there seems to have been trouble almost from the start. No sooner had the monks arrived at Stocking than two brothers de Stuteville claimed the lands given by de Mowbray. Robert Daiville "much hindered the monks' labours" and disputed their right to the land. The abbot was so sorely tried that he "crossed to Normandy" to put his case to the king's court. The brothers were ordered to cease molesting the monks and settled the dispute by placing one, "a certain knife" and the other, "his charter" on the high altar at Stocking. Just to make sure de Mowbray had raised "a great ditch between the soil given to the monks and the soil of Robert Daiville".

Byland Abbey

Stocking was home to monks for thirty years but most of that time was spent felling trees, clearing tracts of moorland, draining marshes and building living quarters and a church for their final move. On the 31st October 1177 a band of monks, clad in the unbleached white of the Cistercian order, came to what we know as Byland Abbey.

It may be noted that, apart from vills such as Wildon, much of the territory so liberally offered to the monks was part of the vast area laid waste by William the Conqueror, unproductive and largely uninhabited. The final site of the abbey was not the area of romantic beauty we see today. It was low-lying and inhospitable in a wet season. Abbot Philip wrote that the monks began "by long and wide ditches to draw off the abundance of water from the marches". Mr. J. McDonnell and Dom M.R. Everest, OSB, have published the results of research of this labour. Most streams were diverted and rechannelled to flow south and south-west. The Holbeck was directed to the west of the abbey feeding a pond and then south in a man-made channel, Long Beck, to the fish pond of Newburgh Priory and then to Elphin Beck. Watermills for corn were built at Byland and Newburgh to make use of the stream.

As well as supplying drinking water, water for corn mills and for sewage disposal, an important aspect of water control was the building of ponds for fish. Cistercians were mainly vegetarians, enjoying fish, in the early years, as a feast-day treat. Later, fish became a more essential part of their diet. Mr McDonnell has made a separate study of the Byland Abbey pond system of the twelfth and thirteen centuries. He has identified two fish ponds of considerable size - a fifty acre pond above High Kilburn that Robert Daiville claimed back at some time before 1190 and another, built to replace the first, about a mile to the south-east. This was pond of forty-five acres, half on land belonging to Daiville and half to Thomas Colville of Coxwold.

It took the monks about forty years to draw up an agreement to build the replacement pond, and even then it was not ready for the fish for another ten years. From the Oldstead road it is still possible to see signs of a series of ponds,

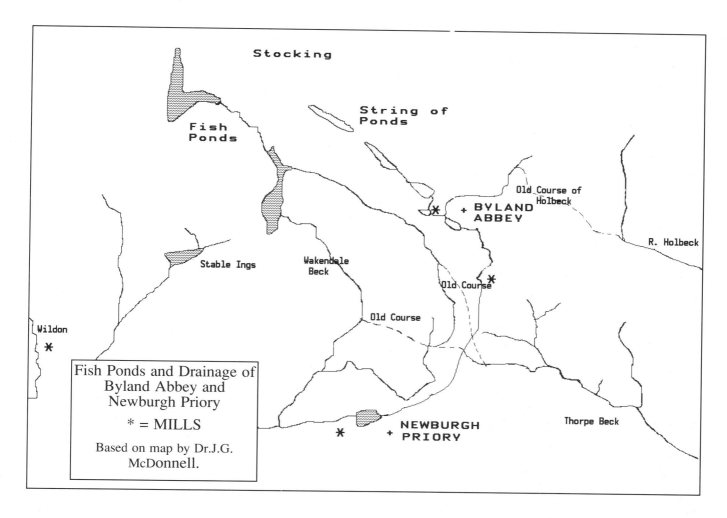

Fish Ponds and Drainage of Byland Abbey and Newburgh Priory

* = MILLS

Based on map by Dr.J.G. McDonnell.

possibly, according to Mr. McDonnell, used as hatcheries.

In 1322 the Battle of Byland took place on Blackhow Moor on the hillside above Byland.. Edward II having been on an unsuccessful raid against the Scots with Robert Bruce further north camped his army on the moor and sought shelter for the night at the abbey. The Scots caught up with the party and inflicted a heavy defeat. When Edward heard of this he fled to York leaving the abbey to be pillaged and the North unprotected.

The Lay Brothers

The Cistercian way of life had a profound effect or the economy of the North of England. Because the monks were to be self supporting and because at first their rule forbade them to hire labour, a relatively new vocation to the religious life was introduced - that of the lay brother or conversus. In contrast to the choir monk whose day was given over to prayer, reading and manual work, the conversus spent more of his day in manual work than prayer. The opportunity to follow the religious life as a lay brother was welcomed by

many from the predominantly illiterate population. The conversi, mainly drawn from local families, worked hard, often in silence, and remained illiterate.

Their accommodation at church services was in the first six bays of the nave, at the west end. It was much larger than the monks' section and their living quarters, the earliest surviving buildings of the abbey to be completed, were correspondingly larger than those of the choir monks. It has been estimated that the abbey was planned to accommodate thirty-six choir monks and a hundred conversi.

In 1231 there was a recommendation that the choir monks should not exceed eighty and that no more lay brothers be admitted until the number had fallen below a hundred and sixty. At the beginning of the fourteenth century the pattern had already changed and in 1381, after the Black Death, there were only twelve monks and three conversi. In the decade before the Dissolution there were between twenty-four and thirty choir monks and no conversi. But by this time there was a staff of eighty servants.

The Granges

The introduction of conversi was bound up with another Cistercian phenomenon - the grange. This was a farmstead or depot at some distance from the abbey which a group of lay brothers would man. They would live there for a period, following the religious life under the supervision of one choir monk.

The average Cistercian grange, when the term was used to refer to an area of land as opposed to the headquarters, was between three and four hundred acres. This was the size of Osgodby Grange and Murton Grange (to the NW of Byland). Very often land given to the abbot was uninhabited and uncultivated but sometimes, as at Byland near the river Rye, it was a community of people and some property. Since the rule of the order forbade the receiving of rents as well as the hiring of labour such villages had to be cleared or "reduced". In the case of Byland a settlement was made for its inhabitants which became Old Byland. When the monks left their home near the Rye to go to Stocking, Old Byland became a grange, the entire territory amounting to eight carucates (960 acres).

Byland's first grange at Wildon was a vill. The granges of Thorpe and Balk seem to have consisted of entire territories of what had once been vills. The grange of Fawdington included a large tract in the adjacent vill of Raskelf. There is no record of what happened when these vills were "reduced". In addition to the granges already mentioned there were granges at Angram granted by d'Ingleby, Boscar, Stocking, East and West Cambe, Scackleton, Airyholme and Sniles-worth. These, with the exception of the last, were reasonably near to the abbey. Further afield were a string of granges in Nidderdale of which Ramsgill was the most important.

As the extent of landowning increased Byland's granges began to specialise according to activity. Mr. Bryan Waites has concluded that in the boulder clay soils west of the Coxwold gap, on the granges of Wildon, Boscar, Fawdington and Balk the emphasis was on arable farming. Murton and Old Byland were on limestone soil which would suggest good grazing. It was natural for the monks to use the higher land, particularly in Nidderdale, for sheep farming.

Some granges were known as vaccaries, dairy farms or cattle breeding stations. Between 1190 and 1216 Byland had sea fisheries and a salt house at Coatham on the estuary of the Tees, salt being essential to preserve food in winter.

Sheep

Important as was the production of food for consumption at the abbey, a major contribution to the economy of the abbey was the sale of surplus wool for the export market. It was this, coupled with the sheer efficiency of the monks in managing their affairs, that enabled them to build as they did. Flemish and Italian wool buyers had been travelling around the countryside since the middle of the twelfth century. Having been received at the abbey they would inspect the sheep and their wool either on the farm or at the wool house and make a deal. Byland's wool house was at Thorpe and it was from there that the fleeces were sorted and bundled into sacks. These were carried by packhorse over Yearsley moor to Clifton on the Ouse where Byland had an entrepot. A document dated 1315 gives the expected amount of wool for sale each year at English religious houses. Fountains Abbey sold seventy-six sacks, Rievaulx sixty and Byland thirty-five. It has been calculated that one thousand sheep would yield enough wool to fill between four and five sacks. In which case Byland's sheep population was between seven and eight thousand.

Charters

Not all Byland's charters have survived. Many in the custody of the Archbishop of York were lost during the Civil War. Those that remain tell us about changes in ownership or rights of way, about disputes or "inquisitions". In the thirteenth century the Daivilles were still negotiating. Baxby was part of the parish of Thornton on the Hill of which the head of the house of Daiville was the lord. In that sense Baxby Mill belonged to the Daiville family. In 1284 John Daiville agreed to surrender sixty-three perches at Baxby Mill to Byland Abbey. About that time Adam de Baxby gave Byland Abbey pasture, two bovates and certain assards, one of which appears to be called Myerthwaite (near Throstle Nest Farm). Adam is mentioned again when the abbot agreed to Adam de Baxby moving his mill. Long after

Adam's time, in 1391, the monks gave leave to William Daiville of Thornton-on-the-Hill to make alterations which involved moving Baxby Mill to Byland property, perhaps Angram.

The parish of Angothy (Osgodby) held by de Meynill became part of the Byland estate, not immediately, as Wildon had done, but in piecemeal fashion up to the mid-thirteenth century. Gilbert Meynill, of Thirkleby, also made a grant "of all his cultivated ground which the monks have cleared in the lands of Thirkleby towards Angotabi by the boundaries which Walter de Meynill, his father, had surveyed".

Various parcels of land in Osgodby were exchanged between Newburgh and Byland and in another grant Prior Walter of Newburgh surrendered rights in thirty-seven acres next to Byland's wood at Balk.

From Geoffrey de Nevill the monks acquired land in Raskelf where they established Boscar Grange. In addition they were allowed pasture for their sheep "through the whole territory of Raskelf".

To summarise, by the thirteenth century the abbey had land in most of Coxwoldshire; in Byland, Oldstead, Kilburn, Osgodby and Thirkleby, Wildon, Angram, Coxwold, Thorpe and Yearsley.

Decline

The decline in the numbers of lay brothers in the fourteenth century led naturally to a change in the holding of land and granges. From this time those no longer needed were rented to secular farmers. By the sixteenth century the abbey held only fifty acres close to the monastery.

In Valor Ecclesiasticus, Byland's annual revenue was £295 5s. 4d. Since it exceeded £200 the abbey was not included in the suppression of lesser monasteries.

There followed the Pilgrimage of Grace to which the Abbot, along with the Prior of Newburgh, made a donation, each of forty shillings. The final act in the story of the monks took the form of Abbot Alanbridge surrendering the abbey and his retiring, with a pension of £50 a year to Leeds from where he had come. The monks with pensions of about £10 went their separate ways.

Once empty, with lead stripped from the roof and valuables including seven bells and 516 ounces of plate withdrawn, for the king's benefit, the collapse of the building was a matter of time. The site of the monastery and the demesne lands were granted to William Pickering, knight. In addition he got the granges at Balk, Bagby Cote and closes and certain field in Thirkleby. Wildon and Angram granges were granted to Richard Lascelles, Osgodby Grange to William and Richard Askwith and Boscar Grange to Henry Burnard.

Although the emphasis of these few paragraphs has been on the economy of Byland Abbey it is not to ignore the purpose that inspired the monks - to offer their lives and to build their church for the glory of God. Perhaps something of that aspiration goes through our minds when we gaze on the ruins and reflect on their history.

NEWBURGH PRIORY

Before considering the beginnings of Newburgh Priory as a religious house two details may be relevant. Firstly, there had been a monastery at Coxwold in Saxon times; we learn this in a letter from the Pope, written in 757, to Egbert, King of Northumbria, asking him to restore several monasteries, one of them being at Coxwold. Secondly, from the eleventh century Coxwold was regarded as a Minster

Newburgh Priory

Gules a lion or with a pilgrim's crutch or bend sinisterwise athwart him.

Centre. It was becoming usual for a bishop or archbishop to be responsible for a body of clerks serving an important church. These were known as secular canons.

In 1059, at the Council of Rome, the Pope called for celibacy of the clergy and encouraged them to live in community following a religious rule. These communities became known as regular canons and one group was the Canons Regular of St. Augustine, an order which arrived in England twenty years before the Cistercians and in number exceeded all other religious bodies. Bridlington was their first Yorkshire foundation (about 1113) and it was from there that the canons came to start their work at Coxwold.

Whereas Cistercian monks favoured a site remote from village communities, the canons chose to be close to a settlement and in some cases made their home in the vicinity of an existing church. It is possible that Coxwold church in the early years of the twelfth century was situated where the priory came to be built. The life of the canons differed from that of the monks in that their vocation was to minister to lay people and therefore they were responsible to the bishop, in this case the Archbishop of York. They took over all the duties of parish work, sometimes educating the young and sometimes caring for the sick. In an ex-canon's will there is a reference which suggests that there was a school at Newburgh and this seems highly likely. In contrast to the Cistercians who, as part of their rule, did not accept responsibility for churches and received no income, the canons received offerings, altar and burial dues and tithes.

Tithes were an essential part of the economy of the canons and the giving an important part of the farmer's work. There was, however, similarity between the two orders in that the canons established granges as part of their farming activity and to provide storage places for tithe offerings.

From Bridlington to Hood

Predictably, it was Roger de Mowbray who provided for the first party of canons who came from the priory at Bridlington in 1143. The Savigniac monks had moved from Hood to Old Byland and Roger, the organiser, brought the canons to the accommodation at Hood. In the same year he asked the monks at Old Byland to take over the churches of Thirsk, Kirkby Moorside and Kirkdale in Welburn, but true to the Cistercian ideal, Abbot Roger, refused. These three churches with all tithes and offerings were then taken over by the canons.

By 1145 Husthwaite church probably belonged to the canons. It was about forty years afterwards that we have a record of a certain Brian, a canon of Newburgh, being appointed to the church at Husthwaite.

It seems that the canons were at Hood for about eleven years before they moved to Newburgh. Between 1154 and 1157 they were given, according to charter, "that place in which their abbey is founded and all the land of the east side of Coxwold beyond the fishpond; the church of St. Mary of Hode with land and wood nearby under the hills; the church of Coxwold with nine bovates and tofts and crofts in the same vill and with the chapel belonging to it (i.e. Kilburn) with one carucate (eight bovates) of land ... the chapel of Thirkleby with three bovates and certain crofts and tofts''. It had been the custom for the priest to have a small house near the church with one, two or three bovates of land. This was called glebe land and could have been in strips or in the open fields. Coxwold's nine bovates was at least three times the average amount of land and similarly more than average went with the chapel at Kilburn. Although the glebe land at Thirkleby was only three bovates the church there was considered to be particularly valuable to the canons.

The grant was confirmed by Roger's grandson, William, who recorded the boundaries that his father, Nigel, had fixed from "all that hill called Brink with all the land around it as enclosed with streams flowing all around and all the meadow which is next to the stream called Holbeck and all Whiteker...'' In effect probably from the fishpond, along Long Beck, across to the Holbeck, the area of flat known as Whiteacres, down the gill to the east of what is now Park House, back westwards along Malton Street to Husthwaite and thence to Newburgh.

Apart from lands in the parish of Newburgh itself the largest area of land held by the canons appears to have been in the parish of Oulston where they had six carucates (about 720 acres) from Thomas de Colville. In 1279 the prior claimed free warren (the right to hunt everything except deer) and some years later the prior and Thomas de Colville shared free warren at Coxwold and Suncliffe. There were disputes between the two parties about dogs and deer and one of the enquiries held to settle a dispute showed that when de Colville gave the manor of Oulston to Newburgh he kept back part of it as a park. A century later the prior had a license from the king to empark his wood at Newburgh where the deer could be protected. The deer park was an essential piece of medieval landscape

Relationship with Byland

Between the two religious houses of Byland and Newburgh there were several agreements but considering their proximity few disputes are on record. In the early days, sometime between 1145 and 1157, the monks imposed precise limitations on the canons. The charter does reveal that the latter had already built a grange. The charter concerned "the grange which the canons have constructed above Wlueshon (Oulston). The said grange shall remain but the canons shall not build a vill there...they shall keep as much livestock as they wish but this livestock shall not graze "Berstlyna" or anywhere else in the pasture of the monks without their permission. The canons shall not construct buildings between the said grange and the boundaries of the monks ... wherever they build the flow of water is not interrupted". Another charter marked the boundaries between the monks and the canons.

Some of Newburgh's granges were more like tithe barns where they collected and stored what was due. Provision had to be made for hay, corn, fruit from trees, herbs, geese, hens, lambs, pigs, cattle as well as wool, hemp and line. Herdsmen from the priory actually went out to the fields to collect the animals. Entries in the Dissolution Account of granges indicate also the sheep and dairy farming the canons were involved in:

Grange called Skorton Cote - Grange with common pasture for sheep in Yearsley and closes.

Grange of Brink with Brinkhill - Farm of the grange of 'dayre' of Brink with closes, meadow, farm of pasture.

Grange or tenement called Ulthwayte (near Thorpe)

Grange of Hood.

The same account tells us that Newburgh held three bovates in each of the townships of Husthwaite and Carlton Husthwaite as well as fields, cottages, tenements in many villages in the Thirsk area. They received income from places as far away as Melton Mowbray, Haxby in Lincolnshire and Coatham where there was a salt site.

Records of the priory are scant. The numbers of canons was not large, probably around twenty. But a much larger number of people lived within the precinct of the priory. These would include hired labourers, servants, grooms, to whom would be added visitors and paupers. Sometimes the sound of carts or horses or the tread of sandalled feet would be muffled by the tolling of the Great Bell. There is a note in a will of three shillings and four pence to be given for the Great Bell to be tolled on the donor's death.

In 1279 the Archbishop of York visited Newburgh and reported that the canons were "doing too much building", there was "too much gossip, too many visitors" and that "the cellarer was dealing in horses". Fountains and Rievaulx each had a stud farm and at Bolton in Wharfdale, at an Augustinian priory, there were between fifty and ninety head of horses. What excesses there were at Newburgh we do not know. However, the Archbishop was evidently keeping a watchful eye on his priests. The following year he advised that the canons of Bridlington should not live alone in any manor or elsewhere and especially not at Blubberhouses. Much later, in 1472, after an episcopal visitation it was reported that at Husthwaite they were lacking in service books, there was no vessel for holy water and the cover over the Sacrament was broken. Certainly there had been some slackness.

Confirmation of the Archbishop's doubts were perhaps most evident when, in 1503, Henry VII's daughter, Margaret, accompanied by a retinue of no less than two hundred, stayed at the priory for one night on her way to Scotland to be married to James IV. The canons commemorated her visit by building a fine Tudor porch. A note in the Dissolution Accounts of at least three inns or taverns on the Great Road at Newburgh gives some indication of the busyness of the township at that time.

Of priors we have a scattering of names, Prior John de Thirsk 1331, Prior Thomas de Hustwayte 1369, Prior John d'Esyngwold, all of which suggest recruitment to the community from nearby towns and villages.

The penultimate prior was a man prepared to risk his life in defence of the old order. He was imprisoned and replaced by a man whom Cromwell knew would surrender the priory when the time came. At the Dissolution, in the spring of 1539, the new prior and seventeen canons moved out, commissioners came in, stripped the lead (rich in silver), removed bells, chalices and all valuables. By May Richard Bellasis, chaplain to Henry VIII and a member of the Court of Augmentations, got his lease on the property, took over all the farms and moved in with his family. A letter exists in which he asks permission to remove the large amount of lead from Newburgh, Byland and Rievaulx to Hull instead of London.

At the Dissolution Newburgh's annual income was £457 13s 5d, considerably greater than either Byland or Rievaulx.

Sources

[1] Greenway D.E.,"Charters of the Honour of Mowbray". 1972.

[2] Monasticon Anglicanum., Ed. Dugdale WIlliam, Vols 5 & 6.

[3] Cal. Pat. Rolls. 1388 - 92, pp. 160 - 2.

[4] Dissolution Accounts. Henry VIII. Sc.6, 4546 - 4550., P.R.O.

[5] Knowles D., "The Religious Orders in England", Vols 1 - 3.

[6] Knowles D., "The Monastic Order in England".

[7] McDonnell J., "Inland Fisheries in Medieval Yorkshire". Borthwick Papers 60.

[8] McDonnell J., and Dom. M. Everest, O.S.B., "The Waterworks of Byland Abbey"., The Ryedale Historian, No.1, 1965.

[9] McDonnell J.,"Gazetteer of Local Place Names", The Ryedale Historian, No.5, 1970.

[10] Waites B., "Moorland and Valeland Farming N.E. Yorkshire. The Monastic Contribution in 13th and 14th Centuries". Borthwick Paper No 32., 1967.

[11] Waites B., "Aspects of Medieval Arable Farming in Vale of York and Cleveland Plain"., Ryedale Historian, No 2., 1966.

[12] Aveling H. "The Monks of Byland Abbey", Ampleforth Journal, Vol.60., pt.1.

[13] Kershaw I., "Bolton Priory. The Economy of a Northern Monastery 1286 - 1325".

5
The Civil War and its Aftermath

Anthony Rogers

It is an historical fact that, excepting known sites of famous battles, the impact of war upon scattered rural communities has been spasmodic. Those hostilities which most affected the inhabitants of Coxwoldshire through the centuries were probably the skirmishes of the Civil War in the middle of the seventeenth century - precisely because it was a civil war and thus involved every section of the community. Families were divided and religious overtones constantly complicated the straightforward issues between the King, his Parliament and the people.

At the beginning of the war in 1642 Charles I needed an army to repel the Scots who had long invaded the English countryside - especially the North. But the King refused to pay his men in advance. Frequently they had to wait. Prominent local Yorkshire gentlemen such as Thomas, 1st Viscount Fauconberg of Newburgh, Lord Wharton of Byland, Sir Henry Slingsby of Redhouse (near Moormonkton) and Sir Walter Vavasour at Tadcaster, all solidly supported the Royalist cause (though Sir Arthur Ingram of Sheriff Hutton was ambivalent). Sir Henry, for example, was commissioned to raise a regiment of Yorkshire trained bands - the Home Guard of the day - and was subsequently ordered to provide a guard for the King while he remained in York. Between 1638 and 1640 the local militia had been sent up to Scotland during the Bishop's War, but by 1641 the Yorkshire gentry was refusing to call out the militia unless they were paid in advance. The militia were billeted locally at Thornton Bridge, Easingwold and Thormanby. Delay bred discontent. Discontent led to unruly behaviour and conduct unbecoming. Many men came from the South and prolonged inactivity led to a consequent increase in illegitimate births and inter marriage.

When Charles despaired of the hostile atmosphere in London he came to York in 1642 to consolidate support in the North. Many royalist "yuppies" of the day joined him - much to the annoyance of the local community. Henry Bellasis was reluctantly put in charge of the Birdforth Wapentake troop. He was present at the siege of Hull later that year, when exploding gunpowder frightened the men and they fled - especially the Bulmer troop.

The King failed to capture Hull and three months later he departed for Nottingham to raise his standard later in 1642. Queen Henrietta landed from the Netherlands to support her husband and took a sizeable force of Lord Northumberland's Royalist Army to join the King in the Midlands. John Bellasis was among them. With the Royalists deprived of their finest support, the Parliamentarians enjoyed an unexpected bonus. The conflict started in a small way. An early example was the Battle of Tollerton in 1642. The Yorkshire gentry tried to remain neutral, but as a precaution they fortified their houses.

John Bellasis and the Battle of Selby

When the Duke of Newcastle defeated John Hotham at Piercebridge in December 1642 more than a thousand of Hotham's Parliamentarians deserted him. But Newcastle, denied the presence of his elite forces by the Queen, was unable to exploit his success. Meanwhile, with the onset of winter, his men at Skelton complained that they had received no pay. He appointed more Catholics and forced them into York for protection. He then marched on Bridlington via Sheriff Hutton to plead with the Queen who had returned north - but unsuccessfully.

Later in 1644 all had changed for the worse in the Royalist cause. The Parliamentarians had joined forces with the Scots. They raided loyalist outposts like those at Yearsley. They marched on Boroughbridge and linked with Lord Fairfax. The King sent John Bellasis north to defend Yorkshire but he was wounded and defeated at the Battle of Selby - one of the more decisive engagements of the whole Civil War. The people of Yorkshire were actually pleased to see the Scots. They had had enough of the war. Meanwhile the siege of York had begun. The people in the surrounding countryside could feed the Scots and Lord Manchester's Parliamentary forces - but not indefinitely with York under siege. With the arrival of Prince Rupert and Royalist reinforcements the Parliamentarians abandoned York when Royalist successes forced the end of the siege. There followed the Battle of Marston Moor when the Parliamentarians scored a resounding victory. Newcastle, his spirit broken, was joined by Fauconberg and Vavasour. They departed for the Yorkshire coast and crossed to the continent. Within a fortnight York surrendered. But Slingsby was determined to continue the fight and joined forces with Rupert.

The people of York refused to continue support for Rupert because they had not been paid. Another constant problem was that any sign of support for the King was always interpreted in London and the South as a suspected rising of Catholic activists. A related complicating issue was that, the South regarded such support with grave suspicion in view of the ever present threat of war with Spain. So suspected Catholics and convicted recusants were barred from service.

Throughout the war the Royalists paid the price of refusing to take the Parliamentarians seriously. They regarded them as rebels rather than revolutionaries. While Marston Moor signalled the end of the Royalist cause in the North in 1644, the real and decisive reason for the loss of control of effective strategy north of the Trent lay in the Battle of Selby earlier the same year.

The Commonwealth

In the aftermath of the war Slingsby refused to take the oaths - promising not to help the King and to defend the Protestant religion. For his continued opposition he was sentenced to be hung drawn and quartered at Tyburn. Thomas Fauconberg was the most prominent Commonwealth supporter in Coxwoldshire and with Cromwell's approval he married the Protector's daughter, Mary. Thanks to her entreaties Slingsby's sentence was commuted, but he was still beheaded at Tower Hill in March 1658. Six months later Oliver Cromwell was dead. Charles II returned to London at the invitation of a free Parliament. Celebrations were marred when contrary to the King's wishes, Cromwell's body was disinterred and beheaded. Tradition has it that Mary contrived to have her father's remains recovered and removed to Newburgh Priory, where they were interred in a brick vault. Thus by the irony of fate the headless bodies of these two arch protagonists are thought to lie in the Yorkshire countryside within thirty miles of each other.

The early years of the Commonwealth, following the execution of the King in 1649 were beset with peacetime problems. Husthwaite was no exception. There was so much unrest that the local populace refused to act as constables. John Myers was indicted for uttering scandalous words. Thomas William Kitchingham was fined for not keeping up the roads. In 1648 Robert Raggett of Husthwaite had made a will when he joined the army. He left everything to his immediate family, provided they did nothing to support the King.

On 29th May 1660, Royal Oak day, Charles II accepted Lord Fauconberg's pardon and made him Lord Lieutenant of the North Riding. The status quo was restored. Richard Marsh returned to Husthwaite disgruntled. Captain Alan Baines had owned Husthwaite but lost it. Few named Royalists received pensions - those who did included Francis Lyth of Husthwaite, Thomas Woodward of Raskelf and Thomas Knowles of Kilburn. Charles II was desperate for money. He imposed the window tax at 4d per window.

George Denham and the Farnley Wood Plot

Towards the end of the Commonwealth before the Restoration in 1660 a local inhabitant featured prominently in the confused religious atmosphere. George Denham of Baxby, who had owned Wildon, was probably a Quaker, and involved in one of the many plots. He had been Adam Baines' quartermaster. The Farnley wood plot in 1663 was centred on the demand for the abolition of new taxes - i.e. excise and chimneys; and the call for liberty of conscience. It was on a larger scale than some others and there were rumours of 8,000 men being involved.

In the event, however only the odd hundred or so ''inconsiderable men'' were captured, though the trained bands of militia were mobilized for eight days. Denham was arrested in October 1663 and executed in 1664. At his trial it was said he had circulated a declaration against tithes, excise and chimney money - an indication that he was a Quaker.

The Quakers

The years between the end of the Civil War and the Restoration in 1660 were unsettled ones. The Church had been disestablished, the Prayer Book abolished and the Laudian practices discontinued. There was a general feeling of dissatisfaction towards the rather repressive legislation, and this provided a springboard for the growth of the Quaker movement. They were to be the most radical of the various religious sects, with a faith built on salvation for all.

They did not believe in predestination - rather that all with a will to be so could be saved. They rejected all mediators between themselves and God - thus the Clergy were an unnecessary burden on society. They demanded liberty of conscience and called for a redistribution of wealth - with all the common and wastes divided amongst all. People should labour for their own good, not someone elses. This led to their call for the abolition of tithes, and, of course, their refusal to swear any oath of allegiance. They saw the need for education and called for the simplification of the law.

Altogether not very happy bedfellows in the class ridden society of the seventeenth century. However, it is not difficult to see why they appealed to the ordinary man in the street, the smallholder's, the weavers and farmers. Certainly they were at their strongest in areas where the landlords were less omnipotent - Baxby, Husthwaite and Wildon but not Coxwold or Thirkleby.

By 1658 there was a Quaker Meeting House registered in Crayke, by 1670 Wildon Grange, Ampleforth and Woolpots were added to the list, as well as a burial ground in Thirsk. These Meetings had to provide for the poor and unfortunate amongst themselves, and to see that Quakers' children were placed in suitable apprenticeships. They were frugal in their habits, noted for their honesty and good trading methods with fixed prices and contracts. Quakers left good records and there are many wills. These early records include lists of sufferings.

Among local names in these lists are William Crosbie, Valentine Johnson, Brian Peart, Thomas Rowland of Oldstead and repeatedly that of Isaac Lindley of Wildon Grange. For example he was imprisoned for shouting in Church at Coxwold and for not taking the oath of allegiance.

Between the years 1660 to 1690 there are several records of Quakers going to prison for not paying tithes and for being fined for non-payment of Church rates. On one occasion no less than thirteen people were arrested and sent to prison for three months. Often a cross reference of records can be interesting - the Bellasis accounts complain of Isaac Lindley not paying tithes. In 1790 he owed £80, the following year he still owed £20 and a year later he was proceeded against. Incidently, these records give an indication of local crops paid in tithes - rye, oats, beans, peas, hay, turfs, apples, swarms of bees, honey, wax, chickens, rape seed, goslings, pigs, turkeys, sheep, lambs, fleeces, cows, calves, and milk.

Local Quakers

Glimpses of Quakers appear in records from the mid seventieth century onwards. Archbishop Herring's Visitation returns point out a Quaker in Thirkleby and three in Coxwold. In the eighteenth century the Registration of Meeting Houses showed Thomas Greetham of Kilburn in 1787, Timothy Cookeson of Husthwaite in 1780, Ann Stillingfleet of Thornton-on-the Hill in 1780 and William Toase of Husthwaite in 1797. When it is realised that such applications would be supported by at least three or four other families it can be seen that a Quaker presence remained in the area for at least one hundred and fifty years.

6
Local Schools in the Nineteenth Century

Mary Younger

In country districts education was not considered a matter of importance in the early nineteenth century. There were more pressing demands on children. Farms needed their labour for many tasks and poor parents needed income from their children. Some schools did exist, supported by the Church, or by Endowments or Subscriptions from local landowners. There were also Sunday Schools. Methodists and the Evangelical wing of the Church of England created a demand for reading the Bible. So Sunday Schools came into being, where the children were taught elementary reading and writing.

In 1818 an enquiry into the education of the poor described the local situation. The Grammar School at Coxwold was in a run down state, with only sixteen scholars. The owners of the Manor of Nether Silton, who, under the terms of the endowment, were supposed to repair the school house, were refusing to do so and would not appoint a new master unless he repaired the house himself.

There was another school at Coxwold teaching thirty nine boys and twenty nine girls, a school at Yearsley teaching thirty seven children and another at Oulston teaching sixteen. Lady Charlotte Bellasis allowed £5 a year to a master and £5 a year to a mistress to teach eight children of each sex in each school.

The Parson commented that the Poor had sufficient means of instruction and that "the Parish being chiefly small farmers and poor people very few would wish children to learn Greek and Latin in an endowed school, though the master (of the Grammar School) has permitted the usher to teach boys writing and arithmetic, the parents paying a small sum".

At Husthwaite the school had no endowments, but forty children were instructed on very moderate terms by a master appointed for that purpose. Twenty to thirty children went to Sunday School where they were taught reading free. The Bellasis' and Wombwells made occasional donations to the Sunday School. At Thirkleby there was a school for twenty six and another under a mistress for fifteen. The enquiry reported, "Few cannot afford it". The poorest children were helped.

In 1809 a new school building was built at Husthwaite at a cost of £36 5s 9d with money raised from the poor rates, which was unusual. The school, although built from the rates, was still managed by the Church, as it had been in the previous century. The Driffield Charity, an educational charity, provided the interest on £50 to teach poor scholars and the salary for the master would probably have come from the same source. This was topped up by school pence contributed by the children and possibly also by donations from the curate. As to equipment, in 1810 Robert Moncaster was paid for a desk, chair and shelves. A poker and a fire shovel were bought. Did the children have anything to sit on?

Another survey in 1835 records a daily school for twenty five at Carlton Husthwaite maintained at the expense of the parents and two daily schools at Husthwaite with sixty five scholars. There was a Sunday School of fifty financed by subscription.

Gradually, nationally, the idea that everyone should get some schooling spread. The Government began to give grants towards building schools in 1839. Two societies, the Non-conformist British and Foreign Schools Society and the Church of England National Society, began to take over the management of Charity Schools. Once a school received a grant it had to consent to be inspected by a Government Inspector who would write a report. In 1839 Husthwaite received a grant of £40. In 1848 the school was described as "a mixed school in a moderate state of discipline and making poor progress under an untrained master who has taught here for thirty years, with no time-table or apparatus. The school is neither opened nor closed with a prayer, the floor wants repair". The fee income was high at £40 but nothing came from subscriptions and nothing was spent on books or apparatus. Out of forty children attending, sixteen could read books on general information, though only six were recorded as writing and two did arithmetic.

In 1846 an enquiry into Church schools gave Coxwold two schools, one a Sunday School and another a day school for forty two boys and sixteen girls. The master was paid £55. Thirkleby had a school for twenty five boys and sixteen girls. There was a school room and a teacher's house for master and mistress. Many children could not attend for want of funds. These schools do not seem to have received grants nor come under the aegis of the National Society.

During the 1850s, provided the Inspector was satisfied, Government grants were reasonably generous. However, by the late 1850s the Government was becoming increasingly concerned at the way education expenditure was increasing. It grew from £125,000 in 1850 to £836,920 by 1859. A Royal Commission, the Newcastle Commission, was appointed to see if the taxpayer was getting value for money and to enquire into the provision of "sound and cheap education for all classes". The Commission suggested a new system for paying grants, known as the Revised Code for Education, which came into operation in 1862. This introduced a new scheme of Payment by Results. At each yearly Inspection children were to be tested in the three Rs. If a child passed in all three subjects eight shillings would be awarded towards the grant for the school. A failure in any subject would mean a loss of 2s 8d from that child's grant. There was a capitation grant for every child who attended

school over a minimum of 200 times. The syllabus laid down by the Revised Code was strict and specific. Children were divided into standards and each standard had it's allotted test. This provided the child with a basic literacy and numeracy but little more. Success in the examination and the payment of the grant tended to become the focus of all the school master's efforts. If the school was refused a grant he faced dismissal. Rote learning flourished. The Inspector came to be seen as a sort of ogre and his visits dreaded.

Log Books (1863-1900)

Once a school joined a Government scheme it not only had to be inspected but had to keep a log book. From the log book it is possible to look at the daily life of a school in greater detail. Log books survive in the area for Birdforth, Coxwold and Thirkleby. Sadly the nineteenth century log books for Husthwaite are missing.

Coxwold and Thirkleby joined the scheme in 1863. Sir George and Lady Julia Wombwell provided Coxwold with a brand new school building, described in the log book as "handsome, airy and commodiuous", which housed separate schools for boys and girls. There were eighty four scholars. The master was William Nelson. Robert Dawson was the master at Thirkleby. Forty five scholars were still squashed into the classroom attached to his house. The room measured eighteen by twelve feet. The children had to wait till 1871 for a new class room and then the parents were reluctant to send their children for fear of draughts. The grant for Thirkleby two years after joining was £22 16s 0d. Both Thirkleby and Coxwold were National Society schools, funded in part by subscriptions from the landowners. They came very much under the control of the squire and vicar who visited regularly inspecting work and keeping a sharp eye on attendance figures. The Vicar at Thirkleby, the Rev. T.H. Smith, took over as correspondent at the school and superintended the scholars' spiritual welfare. He selected hymns, sang with the choir and at Easter time the log book reports he brought tracts bearing "printed observations relevant to the observance of Good Friday for distribution among the scholars". Lady Payne-Gallwey at Thirkleby was correspondent for the managers till 1870, set up the choir

The School House at Husthwaite. Schoolmaster Robert Metcalfe is seen seated in front of the door. Late nineteenth century.

and sent her daughters and governess to sing in it. She started a lending library in the school for the villagers and sent her butler down with Christmas cards for the scholars. She sent mending from the Hall for the sewing class.

The school at Birdforth, a Board School was built in 1878. The 1870 Education Act, had authorised the setting up of rate aided Board Schools in places where there was insufficient existing schooling and the school was built to provide for the scattered population in the area around the villages of Birdforth, Thormanby and Carlton Husthwaite. The school was managed by a school board, the Carlton Husthwaite School Board, which was elected by rate payers. The school was non-denominational, with no clergyman on the board whose members, were prosperous local farmers and tradesmen. In 1897 three farmers and a chemical manure agent were elected. The new school cost £1020 to build and was paid for with a loan from the Public Works Loan Board. A precept was raised on the rates at 4d in the pound, to finance repayment of the loan and maintain the school. There was strong local support for the school when it opened under an enthusiastic young master, John Meyrick.

Schooling didn't start to become free until 1891.

Children at all three schools paid school pence. This was probably graded according to the parents' status. At Coxwold in 1881, a tradesman's wife was told to pay 3d a week, "because all the other tradesmen pay the same with one or two exceptions". The master at Thirkleby sent out a quarterly account to some parents. At Coxwold in 1876 a scheme to introduce a quarterly payment in advance to encourage regular attendance went awry. Many parents refused to comply, their children were sent home for non payment and the managers finally gave in and cancelled the idea. The master resigned, "feeling that a master's position is undesirable when the managers give in to one or two unscrupulous men and allow them to destroy whatever regulations do not happen to please them".

The fees of the poorer children at Birdforth ware paid by the Overseer. In 1878 the Carlton overseer paid £1 a month in advance for Carlton children and the balance was settled at the beginning of the following month. At Thirkleby the vicar paid the fees for some scholars who could not afford them. In 1868 he is recorded as "calling at school to pay for the children he puts into school" and to "signify his intention of paying for the Barkers on account of bereavement". "Bendelow was allowed to come free of expense on account of his good behaviour and poor parents".

School work and the Annual Inspection

Reading, Writing, Dictation, Spelling and Arithmetic with Bible Study and Catechism were the main ingredients of the school day in the early 1860s. There was sewing for the girls. At Thirkleby they mended the clothes sent down by Lady Payne-Galway. At Coxwold Lady Julia Wombwell sometimes sat and sewed with the class. Animal Physiology was taught at Birdforth, and French introduced by the Master, Arthur Mortimer, in 1883. The school day was rounded off with musical drill. At Birdforth in 1886, The Infants performed, "arm, feet and elbow action taken to the following tunes, Bonny Dundee, Keel Row and Where is now the Merry Party".

The log books bear witness to the mechanical nature of the teaching. At Thirkleby in the early 1860s the Bible was used not only for religious study but also doubled as a reading book. Large sections had to be learned by heart. Before one Inspection the master went over the first part of the Book of Exodus four times in succession to fix it in the children's minds. Revision for the examination could begin several months ahead of the Inspector's visit. Progress could be disappointing. One Coxwold master, James Duck, complained, "of seventeen boys and girls not one could put down ninety millions, seven thousand and fifty". There were mock examinations with the Squire and his wife present. The master visited the parents of absentees and their children were sent back to school to swell the numbers. A typical entry at Thirkleby records, in 1865, "H.Burton absent, her mother too poor to send her - but coming until inspection". Every child's contribution to the grant was important. At least Payments by Results ensured that dull, as well as bright children were given the master's attention. Backward children who didn't pass the tests stayed put in a lower standard. In 1876 at Thirkleby the ages of children in standard one ranged from seven to twelve.

In 1867, History and Geography were added to the list of subjects that could be tested by the Inspector and be given grants. Grammar and Composition were added to the timetable. Drawing became compulsory for boys in 1891. This added variety to the curriculum but the emphasis remained on facts. At Thirkleby, for Geography, "Oceans, seas, gulfs, bays and islands of Europe were taught this week, also mountain chains and volcanoes". Equipment for drawing classes included "cloth and rollers for scale drawing", and the boys drew, "a cartwheel freehand, a rule drawing of a star and a candlestick"... and a "hexagonal prism upright on its end". Some new text books and readers were more exciting. The Royal Readers particularly were full of lively historical stories and interesting illustrations. Object lessons which were meant to improve general knowledge and stimulate discussion were introduced for the younger children in 1876. Special charts and pictures were used and at least children could study subjects of relevance to their lives. Topics at Thirkleby included, "Farm in Spring", "The Crops", "Dairy Utensils", "Pigs", "Cows", "Dogs" and "Plum Pudding". There was singing too, to the accompaniment of a harmonium at Birdforth, and recitation. Songs and Poems for the year were approved by the Inspector on his visit, practised hard throughout the year and performed for him at the next Inspection. The titles could be stirring, "Hearts of Oak", "Hurray for England", "Drive the Nail Aright Boys" and "The Fire Brigade".

The schoolroom itself gradually brightened up. Maps, pictures, a ball frame and a globe were brought. Among the purchases at Thirkleby were, Johnson's Map of British Possessions and a chart illustrating a section of a blast furnace. The Vicar donated "three wall charts and three historical pictures - St. Aiden preaching to the Northumbrians, The Venerable Bede translating St. John's Gospel, Gregory and the Slaves - and three conversational pictures, Morning, Summer and Kittens".

Two Schoolmasters

The master's life was difficult. The Government syllabus, described by one master as "mere cram", had to be got through and the teacher could have only limited ambitions for most of his pupils who would be expected to become labourers or domestic servants. If a schoolmaster displeased the Managers or the School Board, or was refused a grant by the inspector, he could be

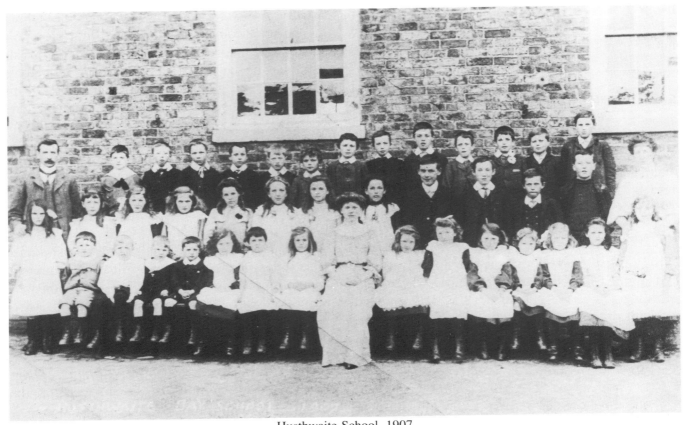

Husthwaite School. 1907

suddenly dismissed. Some masters coped more successfully than others.

Matthew Sowerby became master at Birdforth in 1886. He was a man of progressive views and very dedicated and hardworking. His reports from the Inspector were good and he gained a Merit Grant for the school - an extra 2/- a year for each child on top of the main grant. He despised rote learning and mechanical teaching methods and tried to make the schoolwork more interesting. The Arithmetic class was discouraged from counting on its fingers, and was taught a new method which encouraged it to use their reasoning powers and which gave more scope for the brighter children. Sowerby found Government regulations restricting. He set great store by sport. "This training is so highly important, that were I not under Government supervision I would devote a quarter of my school curriculum to the advancement of the physical well being of the children". The Board was asked for the loan of a pasture field for cricket practice. There was an attempt to start a Kindergarten for the Infants. The children were taught oil painting in school hours until the Board forbade it, and were given elocution lessons.

Birdforth School had in the past employed several enterprising masters who had enjoyed the full support of the School Board. The School Board at first supported the master and raised his salary by £10 per annum. Then in 1890 the Inspector refused to award the school a grant. The blame for this was not laid at the master's door and the grant was later restored, but his job was in danger from then on. The Board was more concerned in keeping down the cost of the school to the ratepayers than in widening the children's horizons. New Board members became increasingly impatient with the master's requests for new books and equipment. The children were asked to provide their own writing materials. The timetable was altered without consulting the master and vital preparation time was cut. There were arguments over the lack of cleaning in the schoolroom and the master complained that he had to pay for the repair of the school clock and for new books and equipment out of his own pocket. He demanded a further increase in salary, refusing to accept the Board's cheque.

In 1891 the Inspector recorded fears for Sowerby's health. "In a school of this description a teacher cannot well teach Recitation, Grammar,

Geography, Drawing and Note Singing as well as Reading, Writing and Arithmetic". In 1892 the master was suddenly asked to resign. Overwork and the shock of dismissal drove him to the point of breakdown. At the final Inspection he "exhibited considerable violence of manner and temper and altogether conducted himself in an extraordinary manner". After Sowerby's departure the Board ordered a new Log Book lest his complaints, confided in detail to the old book, should frighten away his successor.

At Thirkleby, George Whitfield enjoyed a good working relationship with his patron Lady Payne-Gallwey and managed to stay at his post as master for thirty two years from 1868 to 1900. He upheld her Ladyship's authority in the school. Insubordinate parents who complained about their daughters having to mend clothes sent from the Hall were "severely reprimanded". George Whitefield was hardworking and conscientious, he too gained a Merit Grant, but he was neither ambitious nor innovative. He accepted his place in village life. In common with other school masters he acted as Parish clerk and Income Tax Assessor from the Township. He trained the village choir and maintained the Church organ. It is not recorded what salary he received. At Birdforth the master was paid £60 per annum plus one third of the Capitation grant and a Drawing grant. He was given a free house and coals and was sometimes also paid to clean the schoolroom and light the fires. The schoolmasters at Coxwold and Birdforth were helped by pupil teachers whom they were also expected to train. The pupil teacher at Birdforth received two and a half hours coaching after school each week, until excused this by his uncle who was Chairman of the Board.

Absentees and Agricultural work.

Truancy was a major problem for the schoolmaster. Low attendance figures reduced the grant for th school, but also, and perhaps of more importance to the teacher, they reduced the money the master received from the Capitation grant. William Earnshaw a master at Birdforth, was blunt about this. "Lucy Annie Gaines is a loss to this school, but a gain to laziness, and in this respect resembles her brother who reclines on his sofa while others are killing themselves to get a name and a grant for Birdforth School. I

myself know about ten who are like Miss Gaines. I don't go about the villages with my eyes shut, but with an eye on my own selfish interests".

In the 1860s it was still expected that quite young children would go out to work. At Thirkleby in 1866 the master reported, "Matthew Lancaster left school to go to work. Saw his father about being taken away so young. But evil cannot be remedied". Matthew Lancaster was nine. An eight year old, Rosamund Matson, "returned to school from Derby after many weeks in service". Children went to the Martinmas Hiring Fair and sometimes were hired. In 1864 at Thirkleby, Dinah Brown, aged ten, was hired.

The problems continued throughout the century. In 1891 the average attendance at Birdforth was only 66% of the total on the register, though some scholars were diligent and attended regularly, and, at least at Birdforth, according to the master, produced "work of great promise". Agricultural work, helping with the harvest, weeding, birdscaring and potato picking kept the children away. Girls were kept at home to nurse or help while parents went out to work. The Carlton Husthwaite School Board Bye Laws made attendance compulsory for children between the ages of five to thirteen, unless the child had reached Standard four or could be shown to be "beneficially and necessarily employed". There was a fine, not exceeding 5s. for breaking these bye-laws. In practice, convictions were hard to get. It was often accepted that poor parents needed the extra income and farmers the labour. The grant was lost at Birdforth because the school only opened 338 times out of the regulation minimum of 400. The main blame for this was laid by the Inspector on the Board for allowing two harvest holidays to fall within one school year. In defence, the clerk wrote, "if the school were open during the harvest the children would not attend and even if summoned the magistrate would not convict".

The School Board sent warnings to parents of absentee children and at Birdforth and at Thirkleby and Coxwold children were reported to the attendance officers. This might bring a child back to school temporarily, but did not mean he felt obliged to stay there long. In 1890 at Birdforth, William Marwood, a boy of school age, "was admitted June 6th '87, left for winter quarter July 8th '87, readmitted May 13th '89, not in attendance during '90''. Herbert Wilfred, of school age, "was in attendance prior to school treat eight times''. The treat past he did not bother to attend again. Managers of the school were not scrupulous as to the bye - laws. During the shooting season Sir George Wombwell could take up to forty boys at a time away from school for bush beating. Children truanted from school on their own account to go to Thirsk races, to meets of fox or staghounds, to market, or hiring fairs, to the circus and local shows and feasts. Parents were not co-operative. A Birdforth the master was told, "I will send him neither for you nor anybody else''. On the other hand very young children could be sent to school to keep them out of the way. The youngest child recorded at Thirkleby was three.

Illness also kept children away. Some ailments were not so serious. At Thirkleby, Henry Turnbull was "away this week from injuries sustained through foolishly attempting to stand on his head'' but epidemics, occurring every three or four years could close a school for weeks. The Thirkleby school Log Book reported a serious Diphtheria epidemic in early September, 1887. "Four deaths of scholars, Louisa Boynton, Arthur Boynton, Ethel Clayton and Frederick Clayton, occurred during this period and a panic among the parents having arisen in consequence the school was not able to begin again until 7th November, with only twenty eight attending''.

Frozen Ink

When the children did come to school the schoolroom could be sometimes very uncomfortable. One winter at Coxwold the ink froze and when thawed froze again. The schoolroom at Birdforth was badly ventilated in summer. The school could be dirty and on occasion rats were many. The playground was often covered with hot dark ashes, making play difficult. But school could also be fun. There was cricket in summer for the boys who played matches against neighbouring schools. At Coxwold and Thirkleby the choir sang enthusiastically, visited local churches and went on an annual outing. In 1886 the children at Birdforth were photographed in two groups. Each year there was a school treat in the schoolroom, with a sumptuous tea and an entertainment. Prizes were distributed to the best scholars. At Birdforth and Thirkleby the treat was funded by concerts and penny readings given throughout the year in the school room. There were other entertainments, perhaps a paper chase, or an evening of electrical experiments or a magic lantern show. The children went on expeditions and picnics. In 1864 Sir George Wombwell provided horses, wagons and refreshments for 101 children from Coxwold to go on a picnic to Rievaulx. The Vicar at Thirkleby sent scholars on trips to Scarborough, Fountains Abbey and to Wombwells Travelling Menagerie when it visited Thirsk in 1865.

Work after School

Most children, when they left school, went to work on farms or into domestic service. A few brighter children became pupil teachers or clerks. Some went to work on the railways or were apprenticed to tradesmen. From the 1890s some children began to go into secondary education. In 1895 five scholars from Coxwold entered for the North Riding County Scholarships - value £31 per annum and tenable for three years. These were possibily boarding scholarships. Children from Birdforth sat for the scholarship for Easingwold School. Education was beginning to offer wider opportunities to country children.

References

[1] Returns of the Poor. Parliamentary Papers IX, 1819.

[2]Abstract of Education Returns. Parliamentary Papers XLII.

[3] Reports and Minutes of the Committee of Council on Education, 1850.

[4] Return of National Schools. York Diocesan Society. YDS NS3. College of Ripon and York, St John RYC.

[5] Carlton Husthwaite United District School Board Minutes 1884-89. NYCRO BS/CTH Mic 1758.

[6] School Log Books:-

Coxwold. PR Cox 56. Borthwick Institute

Thirkleby. NYCRO. S/TK Mic 1671

Birdforth. NYCRO. S/BIDMic 1622+2008

7

Laurence Sterne

(1713 - 1768)
Novelist and Vicar of Coxwold

Laurence Sterne, Vicar of Coxwold in the mid-eighteenth century, was one of the world's outstanding humorous writers. His novel "Tristram Shandy" is a unique work in the English language. Born in Southern Ireland, at Clonmel, in 1713, his background was one of genteel poverty but with a good pedigree. Sterne's great great grandfather had been Archbishop of York.

Roger, his father, was a youngest son with no prospects of inheriting money who ran away to join the army at the age of sixteen. His mother was a soldier's widow and probably the daughter of a sutler (a seller of supplies to the army).

Early Life

His early life was spent on the move with the army and not without hardship. Four of his six brothers and sisters died in infancy. It was probably this early contact with the army that provided the basis for two of his most famous characters, Uncle Toby and Corporal Trim.

Laurence Sterne © Sterne Trust

At the age of ten his uncle, Richard, became his guardian and sent him to Hipperholme School near Halifax where he showed great promise and one of his masters regarded him as a "boy of genius".

His father died in Jamaica while he was still at school but another uncle, Richard of Elvington

Hall, recognising his talents arranged for him to go to Jesus College, Cambridge - on a scholarship established by Archbishop Sterne.

He did not have an easy time being often in debt and showing the first signs of the tuberculosis that was to dog him all his life. But he did make several influential friends and on graduating was ordained in the Church of England.

To make progress in the church it was necessary to have patronage and Laurence had an uncle who was Precentor at York Minster. Dr. Jacques Sterne was an unpleasant man but arranged for him to have the living at Sutton-on-Forest, essentially in return for pamphleteer work in support of his fanatical devotion to the Whig cause. Laurence was very good at this but was sickened at this use of his talents and gave it up - making an enemy of Jacques. The Precentor allowed Sterne's indebted mother to be committed to Peter prison without his knowledge and at considerable cost to his reputation.

About this time he married Elizabeth Lumley, the daughter of the Vicar of Bedale and cousin of Miss Montagu of "Bluestocking" fame. It was not an ideal match with Elizabeth described as a "fretful porcupine" but she did provide Laurence with his only child, Lydia, whom he adored throughout his life.

Shandy Hall at Coxwold. © Sterne Trust.

Sterne the writer

In 1744, after his marriage he was given the additional living at Stillington and developed a reputation for vigourous sermons at the Minster that drew large crowds.

In 1759 Sterne's pamphleteering talents were again used in defence of his friend Dean Fountayne, who had been attacked by Dr. Topham, a leading church lawyer. Sterne wrote a devastating satire on the situation called "A Political Romance" which brought him into conflict with the Archbishop, who was unhappy at having his domestic disputes made public. He was forced to agree to his booklets being burnt.

This appears to have given him the impetus to undertake further writing and he completed the earliest version of "Tristram Shandy" that was turned down for publication.

Sterne's life now changed with the deaths of his mother and uncle Jacques and a nervous breakdown suffered by his wife. He became more gently humorous and in a melancholic mood rewrote "Tristram Shandy" publishing it privately in two volumes.

The next year, in 1760, Sterne went on a visit to London and almost accidentally discovered that "Tristram" had been an amazing success in the capital. Society lionised him, he was presented at

Court and painted by Joshua Reynolds. Not everyone was pleased; the bishops who felt they had been satirised took a dim view of the books, but Sterne went on with further very successful volumes.

Ladies

Sterne, not getting on with his wife, formed an attachment to Kitty Fourmantel, a singer appearing in York. It did not last long but he wrote her some delightful letters and she became Tristram's "Dear Jenny".

Later, when his health was failing, he met Eliza Draper in London, wife of an East India Company official, who had come to England to oversee the education of her family. He was thirty years older than her and was enraptured by her youth and wit. They were open about the relationship and eventually her husband in Bombay heard about it and ordered her back to India. They parted swearing eternal friendship but did not meet again.

Coxwold

After the success of the early volumes of "Tristram", Sterne returned to Yorkshire and his friend Lord Fauconberg of Newburgh presented him with a further living at Coxwold. With his family he moved into a house opposite the church that was to become "Shandy Hall". Mrs. Sterne and Lydia rarely lived there preferring,

Minster Yard in York, but Laurence used it for his writings and spent most summers in "A sweet retirement compared with Sutton". There he lived a frantic and unconventional life writing late into the night, often dressed in yellow slippers and purple jerkin. Although he had a curate to help with his duties he often gave sermons and the church became very popular, often overflowing with the congregation. To accommodate them all he had the pews re-arranged so that they faced the pulpit. He took great delight in the garden, often dined at Newburgh, and used to enjoy strolling over to Byland to enjoy the romantic ruins. In 1760 he preached to a packed congregation marking the coronation of George III and presented a roasted ox for the feast that served 3000 people. "Ringing bells, squibs and crackers, tar barrels for bonfires, and a ball in evening concluded the joyful day".

Illness

Towards the end of 1760 he suffered a major lung haemorrhage that nearly killed him. On New Year's Day 1762 he set off for France stopping in Paris to enjoy the company of leading French philosophers and nobility. He continued south to Toulouse and Montpelier where Mrs. Sterne and Lydia joined him for the winter. Elizabeth decided to stay permanently in France, effectively ending the marriage. He returned to England in 1764 and to his beloved Coxwold to write another instalment of "Tristram". From there he visited London, went racing in York and visited Bath before leaving again for the continent to visit his family and travel as far south as Naples.

After Eliza Draper returned to India he had another major haemorrhage at his lodgings in Old Bond Street, "it came I think from my heart". He returned like a "bale of cadaverous goods" to Coxwold where he was briefly restored..."I have a hundred chickens about the yard and not a parishioner catches a hare, or a rabbit, or a trout but he brings it as an offering to me".

Here he began work on "A Sentimental Journey" and despite a visit from his wife seeking a financial settlement he completed two of the four planned volumes.

He returned with the unfinished book to London

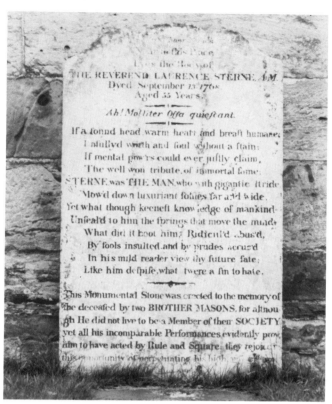

Sterne's gravestone at Coxwold church.

around Christmas time but, while it was being hailed, in the middle of a cold February he took seriously ill again and died on 18th March, 1768.

He was buried in the parish grounds of St. George's, Hanover Square, off the Bayswater Road. Two nights after his burial his body was snatched by grave robbers and taken to Cambridge for dissection. Someone there recognised him and he was secretly returned to his grave. In 1969 when the cemetery was faced with closure to make way for developments, the Laurence Sterne Trust obtained permission to move him and his grave stone to the church at Coxwold where he is buried near the door on the southside.

On the night before reburial his bones were again allowed to spend the night in his study at Shandy Hall.

Reference

Laurence Sterne. Arthur H. Cash.

Shandy Hall and gardens are open to the public on Wednesday between 2.00pm and 4.30pm and Sunday 2.30 pm to 4.30pm between June and September. At other times by appointment with the Hon. Curators.

8

William Peckitt

Glasspainter

(1731 - 1795)

Hazel Wilkinson

William Peckitt who was to be responsible for the revival of the art of stained glass work in Britain was born in Husthwaite on April 13th 1731. His father was a glovemaker and fell-monger. The family moved to live in York where William Peckitt trained to be a carver and gilder and married Mary, daughter of Charles Mitley the York statuary and carver.

His great grand-father was Thomas Peckitt, a fellmonger born in Burythorpe (East Riding). A severe fire in the town led him to move to Stonegrave and then Hoving-ham. Grandfather, William Peckitt, married twice, the first time in 1651 to Mary Percival and secondly to Eliza-beth Myers, the daughter of a local Engineer.

At the time of this second marriage they moved to Husthwaite. His father, William, married Ann Hunt of Bulmer and had six children. Thomas the eldest son became a mariner and sailed round the Cape of Good Hope, the second son George was also a mariner and died in Kingston, Jamaica. William's younger brother, Henry, was an Apothecary who settled in Soho and served George III.

Early Work

William Peckitt claimed to be self-taught in the art of stained glass and indeed there was no-one in York who practiced the craft in his lifetime. The last glassmaker, Henry Gyles, had died in 1709. At the age of twenty Peckitt felt confident 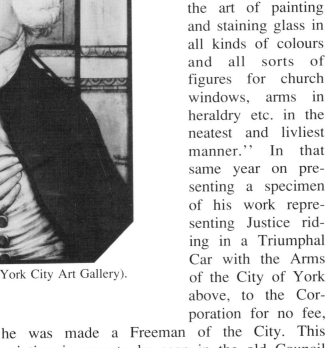 enough to advertise his sevices and skills in the 'York Courant' stating that "by many experi-ments he had found the art of painting and staining glass in all kinds of colours and all sorts of figures for church windows, arms in heraldry etc. in the neatest and livliest manner." In that same year on pre-senting a specimen of his work repre-senting Justice rid-ing in a Triumphal Car with the Arms of the City of York above, to the Cor-poration for no fee, he was made a Freeman of the City. This painting is now to be seen in the old Council Chamber in the Guildhall. At the time of his death in 1795, he listed three hundred and fifteen items that he had painted. These works are to be found locally in York, Yorkshire, Oxford, Cam-bridge and London; in the Minster, in cathedrals, churches, chapels and private houses.

William Peckitt. (Courtesy York City Art Gallery).

The Peckitt Family Tree

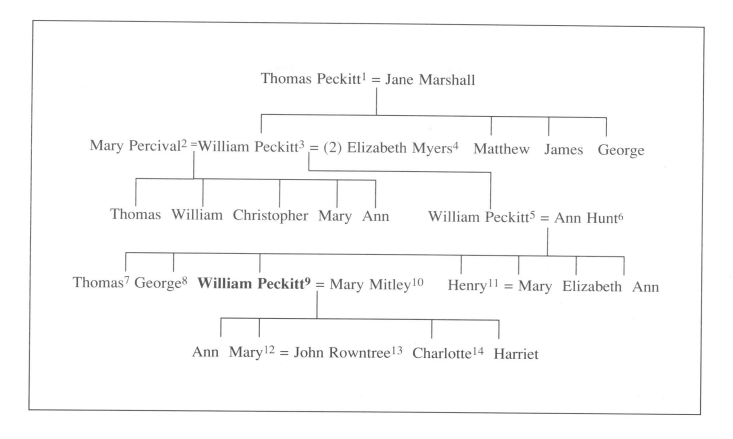

Thomas Peckitt[1] = Jane Marshall

Mary Percival[2] = William Peckitt[3] = (2) Elizabeth Myers[4]   Matthew   James   George

Thomas   William   Christopher   Mary   Ann   William Peckitt[5] = Ann Hunt[6]

Thomas[7]   George[8]   **William Peckitt[9]** = Mary Mitley[10]   Henry[11] = Mary   Elizabeth   Ann

Ann   Mary[12] = John Rowntree[13]   Charlotte[14]   Harriet

NOTES

[1] Fellmonger of Bureythorpe in the East Riding. When the town was severely damaged by fire, he came to live at Stonegrave, near Hovingham and later at Hovingham (c.1630).

[2] Married 1651

[3] Fellmonger of Hovingham. Born 1635. On his second marriage he came to live at Husthwaite. Died 1715.

[4] Daughter of John Myers, an "ingenious" engineer, known as the "great deviser".

[5] Fellmonger and Glover of Husthwaite. Born November 1690. Died August 24th 1774.

[6] Daughter of Mr. Hunt of Bulmer. Born October 17th 1690. Died November 22nd 1787.

[7] Mariner. Born 12th September 1720 at Husthwaite. Died Cape of Good Hope in 1748. Unmarried.

[8] Mariner. Born at Husthwaite October 25th 1725. Died Kingston, Jamaica, 1748. Unmarried.

[9] Glass Painter, born at Husthwaite, April 13th 1731. Settled in York. Died there 14th October 1795. Buried in chancel of St. Martin cum Gregory where there is a memorial window.

[10] Daughter of Charles Mitley, statuary and carver of York. Born 1743 in Davy Hall, York. Married 3rd April 1763 in St. Michael le Belfrey. Died 11th January 1826.

[11] Born 14th July 1734 in Husthwaite. Settled in Compton Street, Soho. Apothecary to George III.

[12] Born in Davy Hall 12th October 1776. Died 1st April 1847. Buried in Oldham, Lancs.

[13] Attourney at Law. Married 21st April 1792.

[14] Born in Davy Hall 14th November, 1770. Died, unmarried 14th April, 1790. Painted Glass Memorial Window in St. Martin cum Gregory.

William Peckitt Window in York Guildhall.

"The Arms of the City of York above Justice in the Triumphal Car."

(Courtesy York City Art Gallery)

Reintroduction of Craft

Some say Peckitt learnt his craft from William Price of London, where his brother and sister went to live; others that he learnt from the work of Henry Gyles, whose house in Micklegate Peckitt occupied before his marriage in 1763. However he acquired his skills Peckitt reintroduced an art form which had lain dormant for one hundred years both improving and rejuvenating it. Louis X111 had been responsible for its demise in France, when in 1633 he ordered the total destruction of Lorraine, an area responsible for the supply of coloured glass to the whole of Europe, as retribution for the opposition of Charles of Lorraine to Louis' armies. As a result of there being no coloured glass, glass painters had to experiment with painting a layer of enamel on plain glass - a poor substitute at best

for the depth and richness of coloured glass. The result was that by 1774 there was no glass painter in Paris.

Meanwhile, in Britain, Peckitt and his contemporaries, Egington, John Pearson and Thomas Jervais, were experimenting with ways in which to make coloured glass. The critics of the time could see nothing wrong with the old enameled glass such as the Egington windows at Magdalen but we owe a debt to Peckitt who, despite his critics, realised that the true beauty of glass painting lies in the effect that can be produced by rich, gorgeous and transparent glass which is impossible to achieve from plain glass covered in a coloured enamel.

Important Clients

In 1754 he made a Figure of St Peter for the

south transept of York Minster. In 1768 it was removed and replaced with another. Other works for the Minster were completed in 1757, 1758 and 1793. In 1761 he began the first of several works for Horace Walpole at Strawberry Hill in London. Peckitt was particularly accomplished in representing Coats of Arms and depicting Heraldry. He was not a good draughtsman and most of his work is copied from another artist. The cartoons of Sir James Thornhill were used for the figures in the Great West window of Exeter Cathedral and the figure of St Peter mentioned above. In fact the west window at New College, Oxford was based on his own drawings and the College authorities were so disappointed that they would only commision other work from him if he agreed to use an acceptable artist for the cartoons. Ultimately it was the Italian, Biagio Rebecca, an associate of the Royal Academy who drew the twenty-four figures which are still to be seen in Peckitt's windows. The association with Rebecca continued when Sir John Griffin commissioned Peckittt to paint from the Italian cartoons the Adoration of the Magi and the Last Supper in 1772 for his new Chapel in the gothic style at Audley End, perhaps Peckitt's best work.

Peckitt was innovative and experimented to improve the colours of his glass. It was something of a mystery where he obtained his sheets of evenly coloured glass, but it was almost certainly from Stourbridge. He wished to achieve a good ruby coloured glass to use instead of the "flash ruby" - a layer of enamel on white glass. He probably worked with Dr John Wall who founded the Worcester China works in 1751. A window in the chapel of Oriel College Oxford signed by Peckitt in 1767 was from a cartoon drawn by John Wall and it is quite possible that they collaborated on other works.

Peckitt also experimented with engraving on glass. A clear glass was coated with a yellow stain or coloured glass and then the surface was cut away to reveal the coloured glass beneath. He patented this technique in 1780. Some of his engraved windows are preserved in the V&A and a number of his engraved drinking glasses are in the Yorkshire Museum.

Marriage

After his marriage Peckitt moved to Cumberland Row (now New Street) into one of five houses which are now solicitors premises. He and his wife, who helped and supported him in his work, had four daughters, Mary who married an attorney, John Rowntree; Anne who died aged one; Charlotte who died aged twenty and Harriet who lived till she was ninety. A memorial window in the church of St Martin-cum-Gregory representing Hope, commemorates them. Shortly before his death he moved to an extensive property in Friars Wall which had been left to him in the will of Thomas Rawson. The site had previously been occupied by the Friars Minors monastery and had fifty-six yards of river frontage. It had three large houses, two gardens and a brick built summerhouse which is the only part which remains, the rest having been sold by Miss Peckitt and is now covered by Peckitt and Tower streets. The summerhouse has some of Peckitt's glass in the door depicting George III as well as a most beautifully executed plaster ceiling.

Peckitt also developed an interest in God and Divinity towards the end of his life. He wrote several works on the subject though none gained any acclaim. One entitled "The Wonderful Love of God to Man or Heaven Opened on Earth" was published in 1794 and is in the York Minster Library. His widow, who survived him by thirty-one years, erected a window in the north aisle of the church of St Martin-cum-Gregory to his memory, representing a large funeral urn with the inscription to "William Peckitt of this City, Glass Painter and Stainer, who died 14th October 1795, aged sixty four, and whose remains are deposited in the Chancel. He was a most affectionate husband, Tender Parent and Pious Christian".

References

{1} Brightson Thomas. "William Peckitt, the greatest of the Georgian Glasspainters", York Georgian Society Annual Report 1967 - 8.

[2] Knowles J.A., "William Peckittt, Glass-Painter"., Walpole Society. Vol 17, 1929.

[3] Brighton J.T., "William Peckitt and portraiture on glass". York City Art Gallery Bulletin. Jan. 1984. Vol. XXXIV. No.126.

9
Agricultural Matters

Jane Rogers

Summer is icumen in

Lhude sing cuccu!

Groweth sed, and bloweth med

And springth the wude nu.

The cuckoo song of 1250 heralds the welcome sound of summer and the new life it brings. An unchanging pattern of rural life tied one would think to the seasons. Yet over the last 700 years profound changes have taken place in Coxwoldshire agriculture. From the open fields and common grazing lands which existed before 1086 has evolved a landscape of closes held in severalty which is familiar to us today. Associated with this there have been great changes in technology, with ox teams giving way to horses and then tractors, together with an increasing diversity in crops.

It must not be thought that these changes were always made because of profitable "improvement" or fluctuating tastes. Often outside factors beyond anyone's control played a large part. From Saxon times until the thirteenth century, throughout the country as a whole, it was warmer and conditions for arable farming were very good. From then it became gradually colder and wetter, so that within a hundred years harvest failures were in a ratio of one in three. Add to this the Black Death (due to the Plague) in 1349 when the population was decimated, a decline in cereal production was understandable. Incidently it left the agricultural workforce in a position of strength, able to command high wages. This in turn led to the development of pastoral farming.

The mid-fifteenth century saw a large demand for wool due to the expanding textile trade. The division of the great monastic holdings after the

Dissolution of the Monasteries led to a reorganisation of farming holdings and the growth of some larger estates. Always still affected by periods of prosperity or slump, by the invention of new machinery, or the planting of new crops - the countryside itself would not have appeared too unfamiliar to us as we travelled through it.

New Techniques

The strip system gradually gave way as land was enclosed. New crops - roots and grasses - drainage and irrigation all played their part in altering the landscape. Enclosed land meant that sheep could be folded on it and increase its fertility by their manuring. Land improved by drainage gave a longer growing season, plus the improved root vegetable diet meant that cattle could be fed over a longer period.

From 1750 the rapid rise in the population of the country led to increased food production. Improved transport systems enabled wider markets to be serviced. A labour shortage in the countryside developed in the 1850s as people left to work in the towns and this prompted the introduction of new machinery. The same period saw a great interest in the improvement of animal breeding and the growth of mixed farming. A time of slumps and booms that led to severe price fluctuations - a characteristic that has existed up to the present. Certainly the last hundred years have seen two periods of acute depression. The last thirty years have been another time of change with the rapid growth in the use of artificial fertilisers and of intensive animal rearing. However, now farming is again at the cross roads so let us see how it has reacted in the past to all the changes.

Mrs. Lucy Barnett (Knee) with tractor and flax puller.

Woodland

In Domesday Book we are told that Hugh Son of Baldric had four ploughs and fifty-four villeins having twenty-nine ploughs, and that this land covered nine leagues in length and four in breadth. His holdings spread over Coxwold, ''Ireton'' (Yearsley), Ampleforth, Thirkleby, Osgodby and Baxby. In much the same area the Archbishop had nineteen caructates and seven ploughs but they are described as ''waste'', and in the land that the King held there were four villein ''but they plough not''. So it looks as if some land is being ploughed and that the whole area has not been affected by the Harrowing of the North after Norman Conquest. Other Domesday extracts suggest that ''Coxwoldshire'' was a much more heavily wooded than many surrounding areas of Yorkshire. To the south was the forest of Galtres that went up to the walls of York. Baxby and Husthwaite appeared to share a common wood on the boundary with Boscar Grange. Words which indicate woodland, such as hag, spring, (both coppice woods) rudding, busk and skew all occur locally. In the fifteenth century wood went from Carlton and Husthwaite to repair York Minster. In 1478 and 1516 between a hundred and two hundred planks at a time were sent to York by river - perhaps first by road to Boroughbridge. However, at the Dissolution there was not a lot of woodland left and there was even less a hundred years later.

As the woodlands were cleared then the open-fields developed. Thirkleby and Thornton certainly had their open fields. A deed of 1414 refers to the Common Land of Thornton and in 1486 the East Common Field is mentioned.

Fields and Crops

Chapter Two has already examined evidence for the form and distribution of the enclosures which came into existence after the clearance of woodland and the draining of marshes between the thirteenth and seventeenth centuries. Enclosure seems to have been by agreement and earlier than many other parts of the country, rather than formal Act of Parliament. Certainly Thornton had two enclosed fields, Short Kirkgate and Broadends by 1414 and five more by the end of the century. In 1613 there is a letter from Henry Bellasis to Trinity College about the proposed enclosure of about 600 acres at Husthwaite

Common..."this township belongs to a prebend of York, Dr. Morton, Dean of Winchester, his tenants are many of them copy holders do agree to this enclosure, in which consent all householders and cottagers do fall on proportion of certain acres - the least cottagers eight acres". Certainly by the sixteenth century many of our townships contained four, five or more patches of open field, each having its own name followed by suffixes such as "field", "flatt", "furlong" or "acres". In 1557 we learn from James Kytchingham of Carlton Husthwaite then aged fifty that, *"lands belonging to Husthwaite and Baxby doth lie in the fields called High Field...In West Field and likewise in Acres Field and in another field called Arterby field...Tenants of Husthwaite and Baxby haith bite of mouth together with there cattell in fields aforesaid and also in the commons called Husthwaite woods and commons"* .[1]

Clearly four fragments of open field remained in which the tenants still retained grazing rights in the fallow year, but we cannot presume that in the sixteenth century Husthwaite and Baxby had some form of four field system, because in other documents up to 1780 other fields are also referred to in Husthwaite, all of which can be located accurately by means of field names on the nineteenth century tithe map. Thus we have Lea Field and a Knapperton Field - the latter containing a number of strips of headlands right up to 1780 [8].

A well defined strip system as shown in the glebe returns for Thirkleby in 1649 with arable land held in strips in Barge Field, Brigg Field, Busk Field, Mill Field, Kirke Field and Westfield.

Another set of Tithe cause papers dated 1584 give a very vivid description of how the corn was cut and the tithe corn selected... *"known the laudable custom that every man having any the corne and especially otes or haver ought after shearing the corn to bynde the same into sheaves as well the tenth part as the rest...to stook the same and to put ten sheaves in everie stook then at the leading of the said stowkes they ought by custom to leave everie first, second, third, and fourth stook one sheaf called a corner sheaf for the tieth, or other sheaf standing upon the ground supporting the howde sheafe and at the leading of everie fifth stowke they ought to leave a hoode sheaf..." "Thomas Holme of Husthwaite webster aged 58...at the last harvest helped lead 8 loads of rye forth of Husthwaite field called Highfield which were truly tithed because he did caste forth every 1tenh sheaf..."* [2].

By the end of the eighteenth century there is plentiful evidence in the Newburgh accounts of the "new husbandry". In 1729 twenty-six lbs of turnip seed was purchased, and as early as 1694 there is a mention in the memorandum book that "I bought Robert Walker's rape seed". Rape was important - it was used to make oil for lighting, as cattle feed and in the wool industry. In 1727 as many as seven horse loads of potatoes were being brought down to Newburgh from "off the moor" and in 1800 the tithe returns of all the villages list wheat, barley, oats, beans, turnips and potatoes. A certain percentage of the land is still fallow, whereas by 1814 clover and rye have been added to the list and the fallow has practically disappeared. One wonders whether this is just due to a greater awareness of new rotations or just because of the high prices for all agricultural products brought about by the Napoleonic Wars.

After the Napoleonic Wars farm prices collapsed and farmers could no longer pay the high rents demanded. Many landlords, such as Thomas Frankland at Thirkleby reduced his rents - but there is no mention of this happening on the Bellasis estates. Certainly local farming was following the national pattern, with the good times and the bad. The next really major change came after the First World War when the Frankland estate was divided at Thirkleby, followed by a period of acute depression that lasted until the Second World War, after which many farms on the Newburgh estate passed into private hands. Now at the end of the twentieth century some farm ownership is changing again, with the breaking up of farms - separating the houses from the land and the younger members of the family going out of farming altogether, those remaining existing with the help of some diversification.

Flax and Hemp

This is not a new idea in Coxwoldshire. A good example of this was the hemp trade - with its

A large load of flax being loaded from a barn.

associated weaving and spinning activities. In the early sixteenth century it was a feature of the Birdforth tithe and inventories mention hemp-garth, hempseed, hemp sheets, aprons etc. In the lists of the Quarter Sessions people were prosecuted for stealing lengths of hemp and for over-stretching or breaking the threads. Hemp needed a rich soil, well manured with the land ploughed in February. The seed was sown in April, and after it had been cut there were very strict rules as to where it could be soaked, as it had to be left a week and it poisoned the water. In a list of pains at Newburgh Manor Court (seventeenth century) there occurs, *"If any rate any hemp in any running water or any other place where cattle do drink, 6s.8d. If any break hemp by the fireside they shall forfeit 3s4d''*. As late as the Second World War a flax mill was flourishing in Easingwold processing a locally grown crop. Flax was being grown in 1783 when a bounty was paid for flax and hemp crops. They were needed to replace imported hemp from the Baltic that was used for rope making and sails for the navy.

Animal and Crop Production

Cattle have dominated the animal husbandry of Coxwoldshire over the centuries, almost certainly due to the dual role in the economy. As well as providing meat, milk and hides, they were the main draft animal up to the eighteenth century. It has been said that if it had not been for its usefulness when dead, the ox would have been replaced by the horse at a much earlier date! Not only did they draw the plough, they also pulled heavy loads of many differing kinds. The Newburgh records show them pulling coal from Durham and on one occasion a train of twenty-four oxen and two drivers brought a millstone from the nearest riverhead at Boroughbridge.

Cattle were necessary but a long term investment. It took two years before they became productive as cows and four or five to become oxen. They then they worked until about nine before being killed as beef. Some cattle were kept for dairy products and stock, the rest were slaughtered for salt beef and hides. There were many markets in the area, notably Northallerton. Cows due to calve in the spring and the draught animals were usually well fed throughout the winter, first being given rye straw, then wheat and peas. Lastly came the hay.

Cottagers would keep their beasts on the com-

47

mon land and in 1617 we are told that on Husthwaite common... *"Mr. Kay fourteen beasts, six half gaites and two horses, William Driffield twelve kine and two young beasts...."* [6]. In George Waile's close Easingwold men kept eight beasts. There is also an interesting will of almost a hundred years earlier in 1525, of Alan Storey of Coxwold Parish who bequeaths... *"my servant John of Brenke a stotte which is at Thirkleby..."* [7]. Obviously cattle were not always kept nearby. A little later the Newburgh rental 1529-40 lists the site of the monastery buildings and various closes. The names of some clearly indicate that certain ones were kept for particular animals - Calfe Close and Horse Close. The Coxwold rents for 1612 emphasise this more clearly when the Bellasis note that *"remaining in my own hand...The Mossle (winter cow close), calfe close (milking cow close), low Mossle next the milne meadow (wintering areas), the long Ing, little close, Lanthwat (hay for my draught oxen in winter). Two little high fields next the laines now meadows for wintering sheep, the Gilder garth for my horse close...."*

As the commons were slowly enclosed this limited the number of stints, and if a cottager had no arable land he was limited to one cow and calf. By the seventeenth century there was no common land in Coxwold so that beasts had to graze, often tethered, on the lane sides, fields boundaries and headlands.

There would appear to be little evidence of any selective breeding pattern until 1610 when Newburgh bought in a Lancashire bull for £5. Usually a township would have a common bull, which ran with the cows throughout the year. The resulting autumn calves would be sold as veal. Newburgh also had a policy to buy cattle at York market in August to fatten up and sell later - their oxen commanded a high price.

Scots cattle turn up repeatedly in the Newburgh accounts. In 1730 Scots cattle were bought at York Market either for fattening or for the table. In 1760 it is noted that Scots oxen were fed on turnips from Yearsley Moor. The January of that year saw a great shortage of fodder because 1759 had been one of the driest years of the century. Two hundred and forty guineas had been laid out on Scots cattle that were sold the following year, but they did not make enough. Some things never

change in farming. Further mention of this practice is made in 1820, so it was obviously a long term policy.

The Butter Trade

Butter was clearly an important sideline in the Coxwoldshire economy, particularly in the seventeenth century. An Act of Parliament in 1662 regulated the sale of butter. It was sold in casks made of ash which had to carry the name of the makers. The penalty for using unmarked casks was one shilling, half the proceeds of the fines to go to the informer and half to the local church. Twenty years before this date Newburgh sold 6,000 firkin casks which weighed sixty-four lbs. including fifty six lbs of butter. The butter was carefully graded before being sealed and sold, originally at York and later also at Thirsk. Locally between 1677 and 1684 there were 144 prosecutions for offences connected with the trade; including local farmers from Husthwaite, George Edward, William Oram, with Isaac Lindley of Wildon who were fined for offences concerning the packing of the butter. Worst quality "grease" was sent to the West Riding for use in the woollen trade. In 1722 the butter market in York was established and butter sold there commanded a special premium but by 1749 the same market was at Thirsk and from there butter went to Boroughbridge and by river to the south. It is interesting that around the time Newburgh sold 6,000 firkins, one cow producing three firkins of butter and two firkins of cheese a year - there must have been at least 2000 hardworking cows in the area!

Sheep

The importance of sheep in the medieval economy is not clear, except that monastic records of Byland and Newburgh show that plenty of wool was produced. At the Dissolution of the monasteries the large monastic holdings of Byland meant there were granges at Wildon, Angram. East Camb and West Camb - the Cambs were in Kilburn parish. There were all leased and then granted to Sir William Pickering with the Manor of Kilburn being leased to Richard Askwith [3]. The Newburgh rental for 1539-40 quotes Husthwaite...*"six farms of one tenement with certain landes and with three bovates and one close called Suncliffe flatts paying annually by equal portions at Christmas and Pentecost and leased to Richard Laund by former monastery for ten years...'"* [4].

Sheep formed an important part of the rural economy during the sixteenthth and seventeenth centuries. Tithe returns show that most of the farms had some, whilst the Bellasis at Newburgh ran many of their sheep at Murton and others were grazed in the park. When they bought sheep it was in April and May and they sold the lambs in September. Often the ewes were milked for cheese - five ewes equalling the production of one cow. This cheese kept very moist. Milking was stopped in August so the ewes could regain condition again for lambing. In the autumn the sheep were greased to get rid of scab and provide a waterproof coating - this was a very slow job with only six completed in a day. The main crop from the sheep was the fleece, obtained by clipping after dipping the sheep in deep dykes to clean the wool. There had to be a fair day for dipping to dry out the fleece and then another few days for the sheep to recover - altogether a week of fine weather was required and this usually took place in June. Clipping was piece work and at Newburgh the shearers were paid 4d a day. After shearing the sheep were marked with tar and pitch - again in November. A barrel of marking tar cost 6s. 8d.

In 1609 twenty seven-stones of tithe wool were produced at Newburgh. The wool packed in twelve stones and kept in a special wool house before being sold in March to merchants, many of whom were Florentines. One wool house was on the river at Clifton. Most families had just a few sheep kept on the common land as the following show: Yearsley Court Papers 1735...''No scabbed sheep or farcy horses on the common. No one to summer more sheep than they winter''. Thirkleby Court Rolls mid-sixteenthth century [5]...''Children and servants to have no more than four sheep on the common''. In the list of Coxwold pains (fines) between 1633-54...''John Moore complains that William Sadler's dog has killed his lambs...''

Conclusion

What may be said about Coxwold agriculture might be equally true of many places in England. Nevertheless the point can be made that the very varied and productive soils found here probably make it very unusual. If any crop could be made to grow in the north of England it could probably flourish and be profitable in Coxwoldshire.

References

[1] Tithe Causes. Borthwick Institute. CP/H 1164 1557.

[2] Tithe Causes. Borthwick Institute. 1584/1.

[3] PRO SC6 HENRY VIII 4550.

[4] PRO SC6 HENRY VIII 4546.

[5] YAS DD94 BOX 2.

[6] 2DV MC FRAME 117.

[7] PRO SC6 4546

[8] ZPV 1/5/2/7/3/ Surrenders, Admittances, Deeds and Papers. CRO., North.

10
Local News

Brenda Duffield

Wesleyan Band of Hope 1906

Extracts from Parish Magazines

January 1890. Miss Grace Taylor of Coxwold performed at a concert on the piano to raise funds for the church. Members of the Husthwaite Reading Room Committee are: J.Wright (Librarian), J.Taylor (Treasurer), J Moncaster (Secretary), J. Hutchinson (Ass. Librarian). Newspapers taken - York Herald, Yorkshire Post, Leeds Mercury Standard, Moonshine, Ally Sloper, Illustrated London News.

February 1890. Churching of Women Fees, 1s 1d. Clergyman's fee for burial 1s 1d and the clerk's fee 1s. The sexton makes a charge for digging the grave. Mortuary fees payable; e.g. if a person after debts have been paid leaves chattels worth £6 and under £30 the fee is 3s 4d.

Publication of Banns of Marriage fee 1s 1d. Licence of Marriage granted by Surrogate £2. Marriage fees 10s and clerk 2s 6d. Marriages to take place between 8am and 2pm.

March 1890. Time for Inspectors annual visit to school. Children off school because of helping with the potato gathering.

April 1890. At the Annual parish Meeting in Husthwaite officers were appointed. Guardian, Mr. Allison Waywarden and Mr. W. Harrison. Overseers Messrs. Wilson, and G. Moncaster. Assessors Messrs. J. Harrison and J. Taylor

May 1890. Annual Inspection of the school at Husthwaite. A new Classroom to be added. The School Board is to find the money for this and if not successful the government will compel the Board and Ratepayers with greater expense. A sale of work to be held and another concert to try to raise the required amount to pay for the classroom.

June 1890. Two very handsome pieces of carved oak furniture have been presented to the Husth-

Husthwaite Pierrot Troupe. 1906.

waite Church by Mr. Robert Sturdy of Husthwaite. One is a sanctuary chair and the other an altar desk. Both were carved by Mr. Sturdy himself.

September 1890. A start has been made on the new class room. Messrs. Fox and Slater have contracted for the masonry and joinery work

November 1890. Mr. and Mrs. Metcalfe the School Master and Mistress contributed to the success of the Bazaar which raised £145.

December 1890. Mrs. F. Wailes has kindly presented to the Church at Husthwaite a handsome brass alms dish and two alms bags. In Memory of F.H. Wailes October 29th 1890.

The Husthwaite Clothing Club had receipts of £34 5s 5d and expenditure of £34 5s 5d.

February 1891. The Census for 1891 will be taken on April 2nd.

March 1891. Husthwaite Coal Fund. Groceries to be distributed to ten widows.

July 1891. Flower Service at Husthwaite. Flowers sent to the "Workhouse Infirmary at York". The Yorkshire Penny Bank opened in Husthwaite. Cricket: Husthwaite v. Coxwold.

October 1891. The Church, after considerable renovation will be re-opened on Sunday October 4th. The Service will be taken by Rev. E. Linley, Curate of Husthwaite.

Husthwaite Bread Charity. Will all recipients please carefully note the condition that they attend Church to receive the bread.

November 1891. Debt on the Church. Beside the amount we owe Trinity College, we ought not to stop short of £25. Against this we have secured on £8 2s 6d . The windows on the south side of the nave are very leaky and the bottoms of the pews are frequently flooded. May I ask the more substantial parishioners to make a liberal response. (Rev. W.Dale, Curate, Husthwaite.)

December 1891. Catechism of Children 2pm. Short Service at 2.30pm for Servants and Working People on "The Dignity of Labour".

January 1894. Mrs. Wailes of Beacon Banks passed peacefully away on November 30th aged 86 years.

February 1894. The Curate Rev. W. Dale leaves the district after three years. "Personally I am sorry to leave the troubled waters of Husthwaite".

Sunday School Lessons. "Circumcision Renewed". "Jericho Taken", "Achan's Sin".

May 1894. Miss Violet Peckitt was married at Carlton to Mr. W. Norfor of Morningside, Edinburgh. Hymn 150. "The Voice that breathed oer Eden".

July 1894. A Report of H.M. Inspectors. "The Infants are neglected and the instruction of the older children is scarcely satisfactory. Spelling and Grammar are capable of considerable improvement. An adult teacher is required for the infants. Suitable desks should be placed in the class room as soon as possible and the Playground should be enclosed. If the instruction of the infants does not improve, no grant for them will be paid next year ".

September 1894. A meeting of the Managers of the School. Among the subjects brought before them was that of "Attendance". The school has been open 185 times between April 1st and August 23rd, during that time twenty children have been absent more than thirty times, eleven more than fifty times and five more than 100 times, i.e. 50% of the children whose names are on the Register have been so irregular in their attendance that it has been impossible to make any progress with them. Here is a fruitful cause of want of progress which parents themselves can remedy.

October 1894. Miss Bessie Chappell commences her duties as assistant at Husthwaite School. The managers are now prepared to receive children of 3 years and hope that parents will endeavour to send their children to school regularly.

Extracts from the Easingwold Advertiser

September 29th 1900. At Thirsk Petty Sessions. Cecil Stockdale a farm lad from Husthwaite was fined 2s 6d with 7s 6d costs for committing wilful damage to the property of William Farrer, farmer of Coxwold, he having broken off four palisade railings.

October 1900. Miss Newton of Husthwaite, while on the road to Mr. Farners at Sunley Woods was attacked by two men who jumped on her, gagged and tied her hands, ransacked her pockets and took her purse.

March 1905. Angram Hall, Husthwaite. Mr. Robert Burton is favoured with instruction from Mr. F Gilling who is leaving the neigh-

Edwardian wedding at Husthwaite Methodist chapel.

bourhood to sell by auction the whole of his live and dead farming stock and part of household furniture. eight horses, thirty nine beasts, 140 sheep, four pigs. Poultry. Implements usual on a farm of 280 acres.

April 1905. Easingwold Minstrels visit Husthwaite. Proceeds for Reading Room and Cricket Club.

July 1905. John Thompson summoned for spearing fish in Elphin Beck - fined 21/-. Johnathon Caisley of Husthwaite, water bailiff proved case.

July 1905. Death of Mr.W.Bowman proprietor of

Blacksmiths Arms Inn.

July 1908. Druids. Local branch of Druids to hold a demonstration.

October 1908. Stackyard Competition - to see who has the cleanest stackyard. Judges were William Harrison of **Manor House**, Husthwaite and Thomas Harrison of **Tholthorpe**.

September 1912. The marriage of Claude Hammerton Rome and Miss Marjories Bateson Wailes the only daughter of Mr. Frederick Hill Wailes of Beacon Banks, Husthwaite. The village church was decorated with palms and white flowers. Miss Grace Taylor played the organ and Rev. George Gill conducted the service. The bride arrived in a motor car wearing cream satin with lace and pearl embroidery with soft tule veil over a wreath of heather and orange blossom and carried a bouquet of white heather, lilies of the valley and white carnations. The four bridesmaids wore gowns of Saxe Blue with hats of black velvet with Lancer plumes and carried bouquets of "Love in the Mist".

February 1917. Whist Drive in the School Rooms. Organised by Husthwaite ladies War Working Party. thirty tables. The Winners. Ladies; Miss J.Moncaster, Miss Margaret Butler and Mrs Norman Moncaster; Gentlemen Mr. W.Harrison, Mr. H. Haigh. Competition. The number of peas in a bottle. Miss Hugill of Acaster Hill. Miss Hagyard of Stonehurst presented the prizes. A dance followed and carried on until 3am. Music by Mrs. Balls of Newburgh. Rev. G. Gill was MC at the Whist Drive.

March 1917. Presentation to Volunteer Drill instructor at the School Room to Sergeant Hursthouse. The local detachment of volunteers was formed in 1915.

1915. Mr.Charles Moncaster had the village milk round. He is pictured here with his donkey which was noted for sitting down in the shafts. The boy in the back of the cart is a Belgian refugee. The selling price was 1 1/2d a pint.

March 1917. The ladies War Working Party distributed to soldiers eighteen pairs of socks, five bed jackets, bed socks and mittens.

March 1917. Lecture by Mr. Charles Turner of Wayside, Husthwaite. A "Tour of Finland".

November 1917. The annual hirings passed off quietly at Coxwold.

October 1917. Advert of Hunter and Smallpage in York. Bedroom suite for twenty two guineas.

January 1925. At the Police Court. A man fined for being drunk in charge of a bicycle.

March 1925. To close a trust. To be sold by auction. By T. Medd at the Blackbull Inn, Husthwaite. All those two dwellings together with two old cottages adjoining forming a good building site. The property is Copy Hold of the Lord of the Manor of Husthwaite. The fine being small and certain. Bidding opened at £200 and quickly advanced to £290. The property was withdrawn and sold privately to Mrs. Dodsworth of Leeds.

May 2nd 1925. Mr. Martin Gibson aged 71

retired from office as Sub postmaster at Husthwaite. His successor is Mr. H. H. Bowler.

May 1925. Empire Day at Husthwaite. Services were held in the church led by the Rev. G. Gill. At Sunday School, the children marched in procession to the war memorial where they laid a wreath of white daisies.

May 1925. Advert. False Teeth Wanted. 6s in gold. 4s. in silver. 2s. in vulcanite.

July 1925. George Dixon of Woodhouse Farm, Husthwaite charged with driving a Horse and trap without lights on June 5th and was fined 5s.

August 1925. Husthwaite WI Horticultural Show and Open Air fete in field opposite the institute by kind permission of Mr. G. Hutchinson. President, Mrs. Wailes. Secretaries, Mrs. Sadler of Tenter Close, Mrs. T. Lamb assisted by Miss N. Hugill. A Pastoral Play entitled the "Stolen Spell" was given by the following performers; Misses Batty, Bulmer and Easton. Dancers; E., N., and D. Hugill, Kay D. Slater, A. Smith, Sylvia Tebb, A. Thompson, W. Wood. Teas served by Mrs. Barker, Hugill, Kendew, Burnett, Batty and others.

11
History of a House

I. Ballard

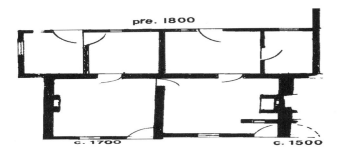

"All that messuage tenement or dwelling house with the orchard backside and croft thereto belonging and adjoining and one other cottage or tenement there and there late used as a stable adjoining to the said messuage and premises on the East side thereof containing together by estimation four acres be the same more or less which said premises are situate lying and being in the Township of Husthwaite aforesaid"

Brickwork

English Bond

This is the description of the house taken from the indenture when William Weddell and Francis Robinson sold the property to John Nicholson of Husthwaite in 1797. It proved to the crucial peg by which it is as possible to the trace the history of the house from the property transactions in the County Archive in Northallerton.

In 1797 the house was already divided into three cottages, the four acres of land being attached to the cottage on the west side towards the village and occupied by George Snary.

When the property consisting of two cottages was bought in 1974 at first sight it appeared to be a typical eighteenth century Vale of York house, with a frontage of small red bricks in English bond, a central chimney in line with a lobby

entry and small eighteenth century sash windows in moulded frames at the west end.

It can be seen from the photograph that the cottages were in a sorry state and needed a good deal of repair and restoration. It immediately became clear that only the west end cottage could be eighteenth century - the rest of the house is a timberframed yeoman farm house of two bays dating from mid to late sixteenth century.

The first clue that the two cottages were not of the same date came from the straight joint (seen clearly in the illustration) and that there is no string course continuing on the front wall of the western part of the house. Inside there were differences in the ceiling beams: those in the original house were high quality chamfering with

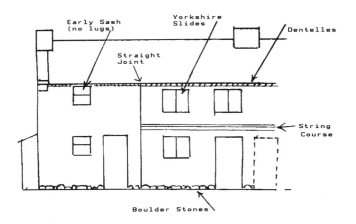

delicately carved chamfer stops, whereas those in the western half were rough hewn oak probably reused from an older barn.

As repair and restoration proceeded, further confirmation that the original house is of the sixteenth century emerged. Timber framing was seen in the wall behind the front bricks when the windows had to be enlarged (on the orders of the Building Inspector!), though none were evident in the western half of the house. And when plaster was removed from the central wall to reinforce it, there was wattle and daub between the original timber studs. Underneath this wall was a great timber balk supporting it, but no foundations. Clay floor tiles were removed to insert a damp proof lining: under them was the original beaten earth floor. The bressumer beam, resting on a heck and stretching from the front to the back of the house showed very professional moulding on its front edge. And the best find of all was in the roof, where a scarf joint was found in a rafter. As there are signs that the roof was raised in the eighteenth century and scarf joint were a much earlier joinery technique it is thought that this is likely to be part of the original wall plate (i.e. a beam across the top of the wall at the front of the house) from the sixteenth century building.

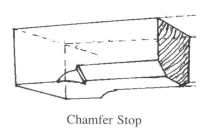

Chamfer Stop

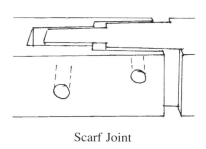

Scarf Joint

So who built the house? He must have been a man of some substance to be able to afford such an up to date style - lobby entrances were rare in the North until two centuries later - and to have decorative finishes in his parlour, plain to us, but expensive and unusual then for a small yeoman farmhouse. He was not the only one either, as there are several houses still in Husthwaite showing the same kind of features. The yeoman farmers also held a fair amount of freehold land as well as their houses and land on which they stood. The records didn't tell us how this came to be, but this date soon after the Reformation, would suggest that they were wealthy enough to take advantage of land released after the Dissolution of the monasteries. Both Byland Abbey and Newburgh Priory had owned property in Husthwaite. After all, the aristocracy were obtaining property and land at this time, though on a larger scale.

There were already substantial yeoman families in the parish - the Wailes, Raggets, Sharrows, the Gambles, Calverts, Hobkyns and many others whose names appear on inventories as appraisers of deceased properties and so must have been considered their peers. But the house described in the same terms as the 1797 indenture of William Weddell and Francis Robinson belonged to John Hobkyn in the last quarter of the sixteenth century so that it is reasonable to suppose that he or a member of his family was the builder. There is only one building left of "the premises on the east side", though there is plenty of space for barns and other farm buildings which have now disappeared. There are also foundations marks of a line of buildings at the back of the house and a large well, estimated to be thirty feet deep, which would be fed by springs in the hillside and provide a plentiful supply of water both for this house and the farm.

The seventeenth century was a time of consolidation for the yeoman farmers, of expansion and modernisation of their activities. Because Husthwaite was a prebend, the Lord of the Manor was a tenant of the Manor House, himself a yeoman farmer and not a member of the aristocracy who needed rents to support his life style, it was possible for the farmers to start enclosing parts of the old open field system. In 1620 we find Ralph Calvert buying from William Wayd of Sand Hutton the messuage, one oxgang and close called Suncliffe flatts [in 1628 most of this property was sold by Ralph Calvert to Robert Hobkyn and Jane, his wife] for "Two hundred and three score pounds of good and lawful money of England." The land is described in the deeds "situate lying and being in the commone fieldes and territories of Husthwaite aforesaid and late parcell of the possessions of the late dissolved Monasteries of Newburgh and now in the tenancy of the said Ralph Calvert....AND also all and singular... Buildings, Orchard gardens and

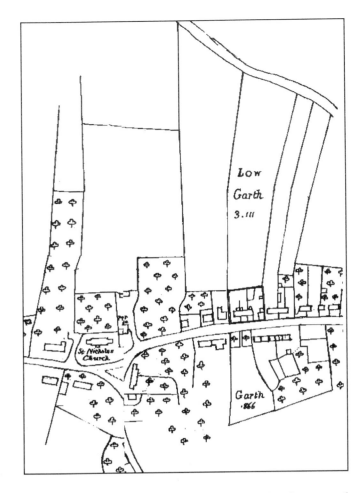

Low
Garth
3.111

St Nicholas
Church

Garth
.866

Tofte and Crofts Lands tenements, Meadows and Pastures and Commons and ...wood underwoods and trees and hayes''. Suncliffe Flatts still exists today known as Sunley Farm, holding very much the same land as in 1628, but in the possession of the Newburgh Estate and rented out.

What happened to the Hobkyn house in Husthwaite after the purchase of Suncliffe Flatts by Robert Hobkyn? By the seventeenth century records of land holding were very carefully documented and cross-referenced but it is difficult to follow the filing system used by what must have been an army of clerks and this document has not yet been found. But there are faint clues which seem to point to the Calvert family moving into the parish of Husthwaite and where else maybe but Robert Hobkyn's house? Certainly the two remained colleagues, for in 1636 they jointly sold a piece of Suncliffe Flatts to Thomas, Lord Fauconberg, who gave the rent for this field to support the poor of Coxwold. The field is at the end of Beacon Banks and creates the eastern edge of Husthwaite parish boundary to this day - history does not record what the villagers of Husthwaite through about the loss of parish land to Newburgh!

Husthwaite Parish Registers at this time are very sparse but some are held at the County Record Office translated from ''five leaves from a book of foolscap size found in a filthy condition screwed up into a ball lying on the floor of an abandoned strong room used by an extinct firm of North Riding solicitors''. These date from 1636 and there are ten entries of the Calvert name, showing that the family lived in Husthwaite:

[1] 1636. Katherinina fil' William Calvert bapt. ert. 13th November.

[2] 1637. Chrus Pecket de Kilburne et Jana Calvert marrit ert. duodecimo die Junij.

[3] Jana fil' Radi Calvert bapt. ert quinto die Martij.

[4] 1638. Radus Calvert de Carlton et Isabella Clerk marit ert. vicessimo die Marcij.

[5] Jana fil' Radi Calvert mort' est 25 die Marcij.

[6] Robtus Burnet de Rascali et Elizabetha Calvert marit ert unodecimo die Junij per licenciam.

[7] 1649/50. Junius - Fransciscus Calvert and Anna Burnet marit ert 29th die.

[8] 1651. Apr' Francis fil' Fran Calvert bapt ert. decimo quinto die.

[9] Michael ye son of Brian Calvert bapt. ye 10 day Febr.

[10] William Fisher Mary Calvert married ye 3 day of Sept.

The register ends in 1657, but between these dates there is not one Hobkyn in this register. Over twenty one years some entries would be expected if the family still lived in the village.

Unfortunately few Calvert records have emerged from the archives but the will and inventory of John Gamble of Husthwaite in 1686 give an idea of the contents of a similar house and the amount of money payable to the inheritors.

John Gamble's records illustrate how the yeomen of Husthwaite had been able to recover from the shock of change which followed the Dissolution of the Monasteries and become men of substance. During the Civil War, 1642 - 6, and the years of the Commonwealth more change might have been expected, but the inhabitants of Husthwaite seemed able to sidestep the social and especially

Will and Inventory of John Gamble

In the name of God Amen. I John Gamble of Husthwaite in the County of Yorke, yeoman, being sick and weak in body but in full and perfect memory (praised be Almighty God) doe make this my last will and testament in manner and forme following. Imprimis I give and bequeath my soul to Almighty God my maker hoping to be saved through the merits of my Saviour Jesus Christ. As to the temporal estate that God hathe given me I give and bequeath as followeth.

Imprimis I give and bequeath unto my brother Thomas Gamble four children twenty shillings apiece. Item I give and bequeath unto my brother three children twenty shillings apiece. Item I give and bequeath unto Ralph Ludlley of the City of Yorke Taylor my nephew three pounds. Item I give unto Ralph Ludley his brother twenty shillings. Item I give unto Edward Ludley another brother who is now my tenant fortie shillings. Item I give and bequeath unto Elizabeth Shippon my servant fortie shillings. Item I give and bequeath unto my brother Matthew Morley that ten pounds which he owes me upon a bond being to stand for a legacy for himself his wife and daughter. Item I give and bequeath unto Margaret Morley daughter to my nephew Matthew Morley of Thirske Apothecary five pounds out of that ten pounds which he owes me upon bond and the other five pounds I give to himself as a legacy. Item I give and bequeath unto my nephew James Morley fortie shlillings to be payed to my nephew John Morley out of the ten pounds the sayd John owes me upon bond and the other eight pounds I give and bequeath unto my sayd nephew John Morley as a legacy. Item I give to the poor of the township of Husthwaite the sume of fortie shillings to be added to the poores stores and to goe forward for them. Item I give and bequeath unto William Calvert of Husthwaite the sume of five pounds upon this condition that the sayd William shall seale such release or releases of all his right title and interest of in and to all that house I now live in. A parcell of ground called Bute fflatt and a parcell of ground called Scaw Carr now in the possession if Master Allan Chamber as shall be advised by Councell learned in the law. Item I give and devise unto my brother Mattew Morley of Northallerton and to William Wailes of Husthwaite the house I now dwell in Husthwaite together with the orchard and garth thereunto belonging to have and to hold to them the sayd Matthew Morley and William Wailes their heires and assigns for ever to be by them sould in convenient time and the moneyes raised thereupon to be imployed towards the pyament of my legacies and funeral expenses. Item I give unto William Chippin of Knayton my horse saddle and bridle and my gray suite of clothes. Item I give unto my brother Tho. Gamble my best coate my new vest and best hat and black cap and a pair of new drawers. All the rest of my goods and chattels movable and imovable I give and bequeath unto my brother Matthew Morley and William Wailes whoe I doe make joynt Executors of this my last will and testament.

	£	s	d
Imprimis his purse and apparell	02	00	00
In the fire house. 2 tables. 4 buffit stools. 1 cheese trough and a pair of tongs. Fire shovel and bellows and 2 reckons. A pot and spit together with other implements.	02	00	06
In the parlor. One standing bed, one trundle bed with cloaths thereunto belonging one cubard 1 pannell chest together with two other chests of another forme.	04	00	06
In the chamber. One standing bed with cloathes thereunto belonging an halfe-headed bedstead and kimlin and a long chest. One coale hole with coaks therein.	03	01	08
In the buttry. Twelve puter dishes little and great, a flagon, a tankerd and 2 pewter candlesticks a pewter chamber pot and five spoons.	01	02	00
In the milkhouse. Five and twenty bowles. A churne, two earthern pots etc.	00	18	00
Four kine	11	10	00
Brasse and other implements. One silver tumbler	01	05	00
Hay (in the Heath, in John Raggett's barne and in the Rookels)	03	16	08
TOTAL	**27**	**14**	**04**

the religious pressures of the time

Interestingly there is a ten year gap in the Parish Records when responsibility for keeping the record passed to an elected official. Marriages had to be celebrated before a Justice of the Peace with the equivalent of banns being read on the Lord's day at the close of the morning exercise or in the market on three different market days.

It must have been very difficult to get married at all. The muster rolls for the period are also very sparse, only one name from Husthwaite being mentioned. Other men must have been involved, but no doubt the yeoman would have been able to hire a substitute.

By 1662, the Hearth Tax records show a change for the Calvert family. Four Calvert men, Francis, Michael, Ralph and Bryan appear on the record for Carlton Husthwaite, each with one hearth. In 1673 Luke Calvert had joined the tally, but Francis now has four. No Calverts appear in the Husthwaite record after this time. Who is living in the house?

Again clues are somewhat sparse. We have to move forward to 1757 and an indenture of lease between George Appleby and his wife Margaret and William Baker of the City of York, cabinet maker, concerning "all that messuage" as described above. In 1662 there was a John Appleby who paid tax in Husthwaite for one hearth and in 1674 a widow Appleby was discharged by legal certificate from paying her tax, also for one hearth. Then in 1745, we find George Appleby recorded by Husthwaite Manor Court as a copyhold tenant. In a village where families remained fairly static, it seems fairly safe to assume the Appleby family occupied the house until the mid-eighteenth century. It was then let to James Tod by William Baker and Richard Wood until 1766 when the property changed hands again when it was bought by John Weddell of Whenby.

The Weddells

The Weddell family were well-established yeomen and butchers of Whenby, near Brandsby, related to the Weddells of The Shambles in York, also butchers. About 1700, William Weddell, of the York family, married Margaret Robinson,

daughter of Sir William Robinson, thereby moving into aristocratic circles. Both these families were involved in the Newby estate. Sir Williams's grandson built Newby Hall, William Weddell's grandson inherited it in 1748, leaving it to his cousin Thomas Robinson, now 3rd Lord Grantham and Earl de Grey, on his death in 1792. Some of the grandeur of this relationship must have rubbed off on the Whenby Weddells, and perhaps explains the attraction of buying a freehold property in Husthwaite, with a considerable amount of attached land.

But by the mid eighteenth century timber-framed houses had become very old-fashioned: new farmhouses then were "double-pile", that is. two rooms thick rather than the linear design of the sixteenth century. The double-pile house could also accommodate two staircases, one for access to the family bedrooms and one for living-in domestic and farm servants. So John Weddell set about re-furbishing the house: the roof was raised and tiled with pantiles rather than thatched, and with the roof, out went the old fashioned firehood in the parlour (the marks where it was attached to the wall can still be seen). Down came the outshots which would have provided storage space, the dairy and pantries. The front of the house was then faced with small eighteenth century handmade bricks, with a decorative string course and dentelles under the eaves of the new roof. An addition was also made to the west of the house, probably on the site of a former barn or cow byre, with a large room on the ground floor and a bedroom over it, open to the rafters and reached by a ladder. Some building materials were re-used, seen particularly in the large oak beams, very roughly finished and obviously older than the eighteenth century. These two rooms were lit by small square sash windows set in moulded frames, with no lugs to the top sash showing their early design. No doubt the many bruised fingers led to the addition of lugs by the beginning of the nineteenth century. The side and back walls throughout were then clad in sandstone facing, decorated with the local masons' finish (a rough herringbone) and probably from the local quarry which can still be seen in the field on the left just before Five Lane Ends. The floors were also improved, in the parlour thick terra cotta tiles were laid on a beaten earth foundation, while the extension had a rather rough plain brick floor. Two of the tiles in the parlour were inscribed, one with three signatures in good round educated eighteenth century script: Thomas Robinson, Thos. Robinson and T. Robinson and the other a message in spiky script which reads "Miss Mary Robinson is going to marry James William Shaw, Tom Robinson said so and her father said so, so no more ... (the rest is broken off so it is unlikely that the end of this piece of gossip will ever be known. These two tiles had been inscribed before they were fired which argues a local tilery; there was one at Yearsley and another at Newby. Given the relationship, the latter is the more likely.

Thomas and Mary were the son and daughter of Mrs. Frances Robinson of York, and obviously

Inventory of John Wedill's Household Goods 26th Day October 1782			
	£	s	d
The puss and appaill	02	00	00
A mare and filley	05	00	00
A Stack of Hay in the Beall Close	03	10	00
4 cows in all	15	00	00
On Stack Hay more	02	10	00
On Stack Hay more Grainger Close	03	10	00
The Furnertir	04	00	00
In the back kitchen	01	00	00
In the kitchen chamber	02	00	00
The 2 pigs	03	00	00
The cart and slid	00	15	00
In the best chamber ffurntire	04	00	00
In the back chamber ffurntire	02	00	00
3 lead bowls in the Dary	00	15	00
	49	**00**	**00**

close relatives of both the Whenby and Husthwaite Weddells: it is interesting that the Christian names also occur in the Newby family. John Weddell, of the 1766 indenture, had three sons,

William, John and George and a daughter married to John Mosey. John Weddell (senior) died in October 1782 of apoplexy, aged seventy eight, which makes his birthdate 1704: he was therefore sixty two when he bought his Husthwaite properties. His wife Ann died in 1788, aged eighty six of influenza, outliving him by six years. John Weddell made a will on 13th June, 1781 with detailed instructions on how his property was to be distributed, also having made proper arrangements about his "Copyhold estate within the Manor of Prebend of Husthwaite aforesaid to the use of this my will according to Custom of the said Manor". His wife Ann was to inherit the house "wherein I now live and enjoy .... during the term of her natural life", and immediately after her decease, his son William should take over, with provision for John to do the same, presumably if anything should happen to William. George was left twenty pounds and John Mosey "One Hundred Pounds in full satisfaction and discharge of his present wife's marriage portion". This will was witnessed by Richard Batty, Geo. Sheppard and Wm. Grainger.

This inventory seems a rather limited list of contents for what must have been a large household: maybe Ann, John Weddell's widow and his three sons considered much of the property their own. There are few records after this apart from a legal document confirming Ann as sole executrix dated 1st March 1783 and John Weddell paying Land Tax of £2 4s 2d in Husthwaite in 1792. But on 24th April 1795 there appears an indenture between William Weddell of Whenby and Francis Robinson of the City of York, widow. He describes himself as Butcher/Eldest son and heir at law of William Weddell, Yeoman, deceased, who was also eldest son and heir at Law and also a devisee - named in the last Will and Testament of John Weddell, Yeoman deceased. The document passes "messuage and premises together by Estimation four acres to the same more or less" and includes "the orchard backside and Croft thereto belonging and adjoining and one other Cottage or Tenement now used as a Stable" ... "and are now in this Tenure or occupation of William Blythe his undertenants or assigns with the appurtenances". In 1795 James Batty paid rates for Weddell, and Wm. Blythe £9 in rates for Weddell. Could this be John junior? Obviously he is not living at the house. So what had happened? - it seems that in the four years since Ann died, it had been divided up into three cottages, made possible by building a large porchlike extension at the back, providing separate access to each cottage and space for a new staircase to the bedroom in the central one. The barns and dairy at the back have gone and the bricks and stones re-used to build pig sties for the cottages, a double privy for the two to the west and a wall to enclose the garden. Frances Robinson must have been a fairly old lady by this time, somewhat daunted by the gift from William Weddell of Whenby, who was probably her great-nephew. She decided to sell the property and it was bought in 1797 by John Nicholson, a farmer, who lived close by at the Old Manor House. He took on the existing tenants - William Blythe, George Snary and William Hayton, who would be very useful to him as day labourers.

But from 1797 the glory days of the house were over; it had outlived its time from 1550 when its design was the latest in modern living. Throughout the nineteenth century it was occupied as three cottages, mainly by agricultural labourers, though some had other occupations, such as Thomas Smith in 1841, who was a coal miner at Carlton Husthwaite and William Frazer in 1871, who worked on the local railway.

In 1841 John Nicholson died and left the property to his wife Dorothy; she died childless in 1853, and under her husband's will it then passed to his nieces, Elizabeth and Ann Severs of Easingwold, or their children "lawfully begotten". By the time Dorothy Nicholson died there were six heirs and the property was purchased from them by John Driffield of the Old Manor on 25th June 1873. Mr. Driffield was a member of the influential Driffield family of Easingwold, but at that time farming was undergoing a severe depression and he promptly mortgaged his new property. Labourers' rents would be very low and hardly help financially. Times were hard too for the labourers with pay often as low as 9d a day with a midday meal and many farmers kept families from starvation with gifts of milk and broth. The Frazer family remained tenants of the central cottage until the early 1930s, when Granny Frazer moved to The Nook. A Smith family occupied the western cottage, though whether related to the 1841 Smiths is not clear.

This cottage held the old four acre croft, though the part named Low Garth was incorporated into Manor land during John Driffield's time. Mr. Wilfred Walker married Smith's daughter Annie, a milkmaid, before the First World War and grew vegetables on the Garth for the family.

Meanwhile John Driffield retired from farming in 1901 and retired to Scarborough with his wife where they lived at Oakfield, Cromwell Parade. He died there on 31st December, 1913, leaving his three cottages in Trust to his wife Mary Jane and their two daughters. On 24th May 1922, the trustees sold the central and western cottages to Hannah Metcalfe and her daughter, Ivy Elizabeth Metcalfe. The eastern cottage with the old barn was then occupied by Mr. Abel Thompson, who had converted the barn into a blacksmith's shop. Mr. Metcalfe died on 9th November 1940, and after Miss Metcalfe married John Henry Summersgill of Crayke on 14th October 1942, she sold her property to Miss Ruth Hedger on 16th May 1952. Miss Hedger occupied the central cottage until she fell ill in 1973. She had modernised it considerably; by then of course, electricity, water and sewerage were available, so that she could install a bathroom and a kitchenette with an electric cooker. But it was a different story next door, now let to Miss Deighton and her brother. There was electric light, but cooking was still done on a very old cast iron range, which heated water in a small lidded, enamelled tank. The water had to be scooped out with a ladle. A cold water tap had been installed in the scullery, but access to the bedrooms was still up a ladder through the living room ceiling.

Miss Hedger sold the two cottages on 18th September 1974, as she was no longer able to manage on her own. They have been restored, made into one house, and become a comfortable home for the late twentieth century with very few of the features lost.

Sources

Wills and Inventories. The Borthwick Institute.

Land Transactions. NYCC Archives.

Census Material. NYCC Library.

St. Nicholas Parish Church Terrier..

12
World War Two

Mary Brown

In the months leading up to the outbreak of the Second World War Husthwaite was regarded as a safe, rural area, designated a reception area for evacuees. By October 1939 not only had the school roll doubled with the admission of forty one boys from Hull, four from Leeds and two from London but Highthorne had been taken over by the army to be used as 146th Brigade Headquarters and the field just north of the vicarage had been commandeered for the setting up of a Searchlight Station.

Evacuees

The arrival of the boys from Middleton Street School, Hull, was for most people in Husthwaite the first major uphea-

School photograph with evacuees.

val of the war. The village school was closed for lessons until September 19th but Margaret, daughter of Mr. D.M. Francis, the master in charge of the Hull boys, recalled many activities organised by the teachers in those early days. These included a walk to the White Horse and one to the Easingwold Cinema (the Town Hall) returning by bus. There was country dancing in the village institute - to become a weekly event - and a play centre in the Wesley Hall. When school did re-open Margaret remembered two

large rooms full of children in the early days of evacuation, a big old fashioned stove that heated the rooms in winter, earth closets and old-fashioned, long desks.

Winter sports were a highlight in the cold winter of 1939-40. Several evacuees, as well as present-day villagers, speak of tobogganing down Kay's bank and the Nooking, making a slide along the centre of the village street where it slopes from the Blacksmith's Arms to the bottom of the hill. And best of all, skating on Newburgh pond.

Outdoor play was punctuated by periods of work around the home - collecting eggs, feeding, watering the livestock, running errands, delivering groceries and to quote one evacuee - "I cleaned the chicken-run and earth toilet once a week for one and sixpence (7.5P); I also delivered the papers for Miss M. going down to the station every morning for the train from York...this I did for nothing". In due season there was potato picking - it is recorded in the old school log book that the government granted children aged twelve and over two weeks' leave of absence for this purpose.

To stretch the generosity of the Husthwaite

families still further, in July 1940 thirty four evacuee children and three teachers were accepted from St. Richard's RC School in Middlesbrough. Their stay was slightly less settled in that by Christmas 1940 only thirteen were still in the village. In March 1942 the village school became a reception centre for a further intake of thirteen Middlesbrough children. By January 1943 no Middlesbrough children remained on the register but two boys from Hull stayed on.

The Army at Highthorne

Highthorne stands on an elevated site to the south-west of the village. For many years it had been the home of the Goulton family, to whom land had been given by William the Conqueror. In the early part of the twentieth century it had been owned and occupied by William Wigram, a bachelor, but after his death in 1937 it remained unoccupied. In August 1939 it was such a property that the army needed. It was a large house, it had land on which Nissen huts could be put up, it was accessible by road and it was empty. By October the headquarters of the 49th Division had moved to Bedale and of this the 146th Brigade H.Q. settled in at Highthorne. It consisted of 69th Field Regiment R.A., 231st Field Company R.E., 4th Lincolns, 4th K.O.Y.L.I., Hallamshire Battalion York and Lancaster Regiment and 146th Field Ambulance Company. The role of the Brigade was defensive but in February 1940 it was instructed to prepare for embarkation, as part of "Avon force", for Finland, via Norway. When 146th Brigade left, Highthorne was taken over by a section of the London Rifles and later by the 30th Armoured Brigade Company of R.A.S.C. According to Return of the Strengths of the British Army, in October 1941 the R.A.S.C. in Husthwaite consisted of nine officers and 356 other ranks.

In 1942 Bert Kingsley, a driver with the R.A.S.C., was posted to Husthwaite. He arrived in Easingwold with no idea of the location of the village. He was thankful to be given a lift in the local bus and then put on the road to Highthorne by the conductress and wife of the owner, Mrs. Jessie Hutchinson. He found Husthwaite, "a place where only a rabbit moved and that only occasionally". He estimated that at that time there were forty men in the house and between 100 and 150 in the Nissen huts. Part of each hut was used for storing supplies; uniforms etc.,

Ammunition was stored in a separate hut.

The following year there had been another change. Ralph Oxtoby in the R.A.O.C. was transferred to Husthwaite and was stationed there until he was demobbed in 1946. He recalls the siting of the ammunition dumps on the road sides wherever the verge was wide enough. A soldier from the searchlight station reported huts full of mortar bombs every fifty yards, all the way from Easingwold to Husthwaite. Local people remember especially open-ended huts on Malton Street and on the wide verge opposite Sandhill Farm. Apparently country lanes all over the North were the site of ammunition stored for D-Day. The road between York and Tadcaster was lined bumper to bumper with tanks and lorries. There was a store of 500lb bombs at Helperby, the dump being built in 1937 by civilians including Freddie Richmond, a young man from Husthwaite. He described it as being near the railway bridge over Ewe Hole Lane. First the foundations were dug and then a mound of earth was constructed, broad based, four sided and forty feet high, tapering to the top, covered with turf for camouflage. This bomb store was not manned. According to some sources, after the war whatever ammunition remained in the area was taken to the top of Wass Bank, which in those days was treeless, and was detonated.

Enemy Activity

In 1939 the Headmaster of the village school was Herbert Baines, a member of the A.R.P. and later of the Home Guard. Thanks to his notes in the school log book we have exact records of several air-raid warnings. The first was at 9.05 am on January 29th 1940 when Mr. Baines himself as A.R.P. warden, raised the alarm, travelling the length of the village street, sounding a hand operated klaxon. On Sunday, November 3rd, 1940, there was an actual raid. Fourteen high explosive bombs were dropped in a line between the Flower o' May Farm and Acaster farm. There were no casualties other than one hen, no fires but some house windows were broken and at least one ceiling came down. In the fields there were craters ten by six feet. On another occasion a bomb was dropped in the gateway of Sunley Wood Farm - half a mile away the whole village was thrown into alarm by the sound of the explosion. Incendiary bombs also fell on the stack yard of Lodge Farm on Malton Street.

Another frightening incident occurred when a German plane flew the length of the village street so low that the pilot could be seen and could have been shot with a rifle had the warden, Charlie Dowson, been armed.

Late in the war a train returning from Helmsley, having taken a party of soldiers to Duncombe Park Camp was gunned by a plane. The only one on board apart from the driver was the guard, Tom Inman, and he got a direct hit and was killed. The incident occurred at the bridge after Cuckoo Bridge and the bullet holes can still be seen.

One bomb fell only a few hundred yards from the village green and was undetected for forty years. In the early 1980s an incendiary bomb was found when some alterations were being carried out in the chimney of one of the council houses.

More regular, however, than the air raids was the sight and sound of our own planes on bombing missions from nearby airfields. Many people remember the sky black with planes, first getting into formation and then setting off for the coast. They knew when to expect them to leave and when to return and the noise of the engines told the tale of those that were merely limping home. Not a few crashed within a short distance of base, one at Boscar, near the A19 and four in the region of Tollerton and Alne.

The Search Light Station

The second military involvement was the setting up of the Search Light Station in what had previously been known as the Show Field. It was close to the site of the Elizabethan Light, Beacon Banks, and as in Tudor times, the need in 1939 was to defend against expected invasion. In addition the unit had a role to play in intercepting enemy aircraft and preventing them from reaching centres of industry on Teesside, the West Riding and further afield. Finally some of the success of our own air activity depended on the protection of our air bases and for this purpose Husthwaite was in a strategic position flanked by a string of airfields. Catterick, Dishforth and Linton were opened in 1939, Leeming, Tholthorpe and Topcliffe opened in 1940, Dalton in 1941 and Skipton on Swale in 1942. These bases were but a small number of the total in the area where according to one historian "the whole

Vale of York became one huge landing strip with airfields every few miles".

In response to all these necessities Regimental H.Q. of the 54th Searchlight was set up at Malton and from there three batteries operated; 411 based at Pocklington, 413 at Filey and 412 at Easingwold. Each of these was responsible for about fifteen sites of which Husthwaite was one. On 5th October 1939 men of the 1st 5th Durham Light Infantry arrived to take up billets in Easingwold Town Hall, followed by fifteen ATS personnel billeted in what had been the workhouse on Stillington Road. A cook house was built behind the George Hotel and within a short time three huts had been put up on the village green. The War Diaries record that on 1st

Freddie Richmond with ammunition cases stored in a Nissen hut on Malton Street.

November the strength of the company at Easingwold was twelve officers and 340 other ranks, many of whom would be engaged in operations on the scattered sites.

The entrance to the Husthwaite site was gated and manned by a sentry. Near to the gate and backing onto the Vicarage grounds was a cookhouse, conveniently close to four more Nissen huts - the sergeant's office with a radio transmitter set (RTS), his living quarters and quarters for about 10 men. Beyond these were the gun pit with Lewis Machine Gun and the

Searchlight. A hundred yards further on was a sound locator. This was in an iron framework with three big trumpets or horns. The men wore earphones and from each horn came a tube to the earpiece. As the operator swung the apparatus the sound would increase or diminish. A strong sound required him to report to the searchlight commander who would shout for the light to be exposed.

The firing of the gun was a more complicated process. To safeguard our own aircraft there was radio communication between our planes and Easingwold Headquarters who would then pass the message to fire to the operator of the RTS on site. He would give the signal to the gun operator. Husthwaite Village was well aware of activity at its own searchlight detachment. The voice of one particular sergeant could be heard in Thormanby. Unfortunately when in radio communication with Easingwold he was picked up on civilian wireless sets and after several complaints about his language he was posted away.

Success in these operation was measured not only in the number of enemy planes brought down but also in the number of planes diverted from target or forced to return to base damaged.

The Home Gaurd

One enemy plane, probably a Heinkel, was brought down at Tollerton and the Husthwaite station was credited with this. It was the cause of much gratification in the Battery and is also remembered with pride in the village.

In May 1940, after the invasion of Holland and Belgium, it was feared that an invasion of England by parachute attack was imminent All military leave was cancelled and the sentry posting was increased from one to two men on each site. The men were advised that the enemy would probably be wearing either R.A.F. uniform or khaki and were ordered to shoot to kill. At first each group of ten men would be armed with three rifles and bayonets on the end of pikes. One soldier at the Husthwaite site was given the task of dealing with a box or crate of bottles containing an explosive liquid. His instructions were that the bottles were to be thrown at an enemy advancing on the village. On impact the bottles would break and the liquid cause an explosion. The same bottles were buried in a deep hole close to the gate.

The Home Gaurd

It was at this point that an appeal was made to civilians. On the evening of Tuesday, May 14th, the Secretary of State for War, Anthony Eden, called for volunteers to defend towns and villages in the event of a parachute invasion.

Within twenty four hours several villagers cycled to Thirsk to enrol at the Police Station. In a matter of days they were notified and the first meeting was held at Beacon Banks. Captain Green, later Colonel, was in over-all charge of platoons at Husthwaite, Carlton Husthwaite, Thormanby, Thirsk and Hutton Sessay. Captain Wombwell of Newburgh was in charge of the Coxwold Platoon. In Husthwaite the second-in-command was Mr. Buffey, the vicar, and the members made up a typical cross section of the village, including farmers, mechanics, a butcher, a retired colonel, two school teachers and a gardener. A khaki arm-band with the letter L.D.V. stencilled in white was at first the only insignia. Having been promoted to the Home Guard, a new name coined by Winston Churchill, they were given county titles like those of the regular army, so our local Home Guard became the North Riding of Yorkshire NYR 1st Battalion. Later each man received a shoulder flash denoting the county and number, NRY 1st Batt. 17th Platoon D COY.

When khaki uniforms became available Mrs. Buffey was brought in to drive to Thirsk to collect them. Recollections vary about the fit. It

Miss K. Callaway with Lord de la Warr inspecting flax at Easingwold (Now the BATA warehouse). Courtesy Y.E.P.

was felt there was no chance of the denims fitting but some recall that the rest was reasonable. Others remember trousers reaching the armpits, a tunic too tight and a great coat long enough to bury a man. The boots did fit.

After the inaugural meeting, weekly meetings took place in the Village Institute and a small station was set up in the stables of Beacon Banks as the Observation Post, known nationally as the O.P., but in Husthwaite as the look-out Post. The routine was that each night one man was on duty outside and two men inside for two hours at a time. Drill sessions took place in a variety of locations, down the main street and in the school playground.

In the early days the Home Guard joined forces with the army in manning the searchlight when it was first set up at Lodge Farm. There was co-operation from Highthorne, too, where the rifle range, situated in the "quarry field", was made available for practice. In the summer of 1990 the nissen hut can still be seen in this field and shells were being unearthed by the farmer until about 1988.

The Home Guard also did assault training at Highthorne which involved crossing water by one-handed rope. Colonel Green was one of many who fell in. Manoeuvres were not always planned to the last detail. Despatch riders were

sent on many a mission the purpose of which remained a mystery. One exercise was to capture Blois Hall but arriving there they found no opposition at all. There was an exercise and rally at Wildon Hill from where Stan Marwood sent messages by morse code to Carlton Husthwaite. On another occasion faces were blackened to meet the senior boys of Ampleforth College in an encounter by a local beck. The boys proved to be the tougher.

The time devoted by members of the Home Guard and of the A.R.P. was considerable. All-night duty was followed by work the next day. Sundays often had to be given up for Church parades. By the time, in December 1944, when the Home Guard was stood down, about fifty men from Husthwaite and nearby villages had given many hundreds of hours preparing to defend their country.

The Flax Factory

For generations fibre flax had provided canvas and rope for shipping, hose for fire fighting, machine-gun belts and industrial thread for stitching of servicemen's boots. During the Second World War it was put to an increasing number of uses - a covering for aeroplane wings, parachute harness and an essential part in the constructing of PLUTO (pipe line under the ocean) the name given to the means of supplying Allied Troops with fuel once the D-Day landings were underway.

The Flax factory at Easingwold was one of seventeen processing plants opened during the war to provide this essential commodity. It was considered to be work of national importance and unmarried women liable to call up from December 1941 could choose to do this work as an alternative to joining one of the women's services. The factory, built for the purpose by Wm. Birch of York, just off the A19, about one mile south of Easingwold, was known as the York and Cambridge Flax Factory.

In 1942 a manageress, Miss.K.Callaway, was sent to the training centre at Newmarket to organise the new establishment. Women were brought by special bus from Thormanby, Husthwaite, Coxwold, Newburgh Farm, Oulston, Crayke, Easingwold and Stillington. To increase the work-force some were also drafted from Rowntree's factory in York.

One advantage of flax is that it is not affected by wire-worm, so grassland newly ploughed can be sown with flax. On the other hand, ideally, flax should only be grown on land after an interval of five or six years. In war-time this had to be overlooked.

To ensure that the crop was harvested at exactly the right time Miss Callaway was often to be seen on horseback visiting the fields and if there was no other labour available she would arrange for the women from the factory to be taken to the fields to pull the crop. Machines were used but hand pulling was not uncommon. The flax was then bound, taken by tractor trailer to the factory where an elevator transferred it to the top floor of the building. There the load was put through a de-seeding machine, the seed being released on a conveyor belt and the straw being delivered by chute to the next floor. As each load was treated the floor had to be swept, a particularly dusty job to which the girls took badly and for this reason men from the P.O.W. camp at Thirkleby were brought in.

On the second floor the flax was scutched, beaten by machine rollers so that the fibre was separated from the tow. From the scutching machine the fibres were sorted and dressed and packed for despatch, the tow meanwhile, on the ground floor, was put through rollers, compressed, baled and sent away to be used in paper manufacture.

Apart from Saturday afternoon and Sunday the factory operated night and day and employed about fifty people per shift, of which there were three. It was a venture that was brought to a conclusion as the war demands declined and as synthetics took the place of natural fibres.

Prisoner of War camp at Thirkleby

The P.O.W. camp at Thirkleby was built in 1942 on a five and a half acre site, part of White Horse Farm on the road between Coxwold and the A19. The land was compulsorily taken over and the first prisoners, Italian, helped to put up the pre-fabricated buildings on cement foundations. According to a local farmer there were about 900 prisoners which would accord with the pattern of P.O.W. camps as described in the International Red Cross reports of the period. The men worked mainly on the land, either walking to nearby farms or taken by lorry to farms further away. A relatively small number worked at the Flax factory. Back at the camp they were well fed and spent their recreational time gardening or making things from available material - slippers from twine, toys from bits of wood. The appearance of the camp was immaculate and it is recalled that no prisoner ever tried to escape. The buildings still stand today, having been put to a variety of uses in the intervening years.

Meanwhile, on the home front, the Husthwaite branch of the W.I. organised knitting for the services described as soldiers' comforts, darning for soldiers stationed in the village, help for the P.O.W.'s (presumably knitting), comforts for Russian women and children and fund raising for the needy in French villages. There were campaigns for an increase in home vegetable growing. Extra sugar was distributed for jam making and a small fruit canning industry was set up in members' homes. Throughout the war savings groups were active, in school and in the W.I., War Savings Weeks attracted amazing savings. In 1943 during Wings for Victory Week £6118 was invested by the village - this at a time when the minimum wage in farming was between £3 and £3 5s.

The whole family was involved in the keeping of

Dora Bragg (now Mrs. Taylor of Low Parks Farm) as a Landgirl at Sunley Wood Farm.

The Land Army

On the land men and women, often the daughter of the family who would otherwise have been eligible for national service, worked exceedingly hard. Because the farmer could call on this help the number of Land Army Girls employed in Husthwaite was not great. One, however, worked at Beacon Banks where the tennis court was ploughed and given over to vegetables. Two were employed at Baxby Mill and one at Pond Head. Miss Dora Bragg came from the West Riding to Sunley Wood Farm and subsequently married the son at the neighbouring farm of Low Parks. There she is still leading the cows and feeding the hens. There was a Land Army hostel at Easingwold on the Stillington Road. About forty girls slept on bunk beds in the dormitory. They worked hard, threshing and baling in the summer, turnip and sugar beet pulling in the winter. Several of these Land Army girls married local people and settled in the area.

Another source of help came from members of the community in the forces. One former soldier remembers that he was twice given Agricultural leave of one month which he spent picking potatoes and turnip pulling.

There is one more memory of the war relived by all who are happy to be in Husthwaite, fifty years on. In the Church is a board on which the names of thirty-nine men and women from Husthwaite, Birdforth and Carlton are inscribed. It is a "Roll of Honour" displayed with thankfulness for the active service and safe return of members of the armed forces. Local men and women were involved in most areas of conflict from Norway and Dunkirk to D-Day, at sea and in the air. Two soldiers were wounded, one in Italy and one at Caen and a third suffered as a prisoner of war but all returned home to a grateful community.

a pig. Kitchen waste was collected and re-named pig-swill. At the manor house they must have kept a number of pigs as one of the household would go to Highthorne to collect the waste from the Army kitchen. A pig club was formed for the distribution of meal, supplied in exchange for coupons (and cash) which members obtained when the family bacon coupons had been surrendered. This was no hardship as the pig proved be a most important source of food and of extra money especially when sold on the black-market. Officially only a licensed pig-killer was authorised to kill a pig. In Husthwaite there were two - Isaac Bowman and William Idell, the butcher. The pig would be picked up in a van, killed and then returned. It was then salted and kept on the pantry floor unless it was destined for the black market. At least one farmer in the Easingwold area was brought to court for claiming that his pig had died whereas it had been sold. Many more got away with it.

To the farmer the war brought a welcome increase in prices for his crops and livestock. There was a certain amount of direction from the War Agricultural Executive Committee, but the writer has not learned of bad relations in Husthwaite as a result of this.

Sources

[1] War Diaries 412 COY 1/5 Durham Light Infantry. WO 166. PRO.

[2] Husthwaite School Log Book.

[3] Easingwold Advertiser, 1939 - 46.

[4] Barrymore Bruce, "Action Stations".

13
Baxby

E. Smith

To the west of Husthwaite village is the farm of Baxby Manor. It is approached by a farm track that was described in a twelfth century document as "an ancient way to Baxby and Husthwaite". The farm, its house and the disused mill behind are all that remain of the ancient township and lands of Baxby.

Baxby first recorded in the Domesday Survey as Bachesbi and Basche(s)bi, is clearly of Scandinavian origin., the first element being the Danish personal name Bak(r), with -by, a settlement. It is believed that Baxby was never more than a manor house, two or three mills and a few farms.

The estate covered an area of approximately 2000 acres, which on today's map would be bounded by the River Kyle to the south.

The descent of the lands at Baxby is complicated and not well recorded.

Manorial Descent and Inhabitants

By the time of Domesday in 1086, Baxby was already under "multi ownership" and had become intermingled with other manors.

The Manor of Husthwaite was originally almost certainly that part of Baxby that had previously been given to the Church of St. Peter, York. Ulfr had made gifts of land to the Church before the Conquest. These are commemorated by the "Horn of Ulfr", an elephant tusk, carved in Salerno during the first half of the eleventh century, and now in the Minster Treasury.

Following the Conquest, Baxby follows two main descents, one through the Earls of Northumberland and the other through the Church of St. Peter in York. Much of Baxby owed allegiance to the Honour of Mowbray. It was leased with Kilburn and Thornton Hill to Robert Daiville

(Constable) of Kilburn, who, before 1190, was also paying rent of 13d. to the Church of St. Peter for the farm of the Mill at Baxby. He was granted suit of the Mill (Wanless Mill) at Thornton in 1169.

The Baxbys of Baxby

In 1150 Adam de Baxby gave lands to Byland including ''Mirethwaite'' (Boscar) and possibly Angram. In 1169 a grant of land was made to Byland ''beneath the ancient way to Husthwaite and Baxby.'' Also in the twelfth century the abbot of Byland agreed to let Adam de Baxeby move a mill to Thornton.

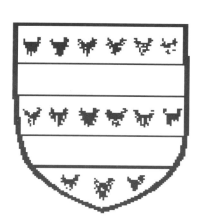

Baxby of Baxby

Ermine two bars gules

During the reign of Henry II the king granted lands to the Manor of Baxby to be held in perpetuity. By 1200 St. Peter's prebend had land in Husthwaite and Baxby. The tithes of Baxby were released for ten shillings.

From the reign of Henry II to about 1228 the reduced manor of Baxby was within the forest of Galtres and the Bailiwick of Easingwold. It was probably ridden out following the Charter of 1279, but within the purloin until 1630 and for some purposes until the eighteenth century.

From the fourteenth century, Baxby and Thornton Hill were combined as one township for tax purposes as Thornton cum Baxby, but Baxby kept its identity until it was merged with Husthwaite for all civil purposes in 1877.

Robert de Baxeby had been lord of Baxby during the thirteenth century, whilst Matilda Percy (wife of John Daiville) was lady of the manors of Baxby and Thornton and paying suite of the mill at Baxby in 1230. After taking part in Simon de Montfort's rebellion in 1258, John Daiville had

to borrow money to pay his fine. In 1284 he surrendered land above Baxby Mill (possibly Angram) to Byland. By 1284 the land held by Roger de Mowbray in Baxby and Thornton amounted to three carucates and was let to John Daiville for three shillings a year. Meanwhile other land at Baxby was changing hands.

In a mid-thirteenth century document Stephan and Juliana de Berningham agreed to convey two carucates at Baxby to Alan son of John de Estalon. In 1262 John son of Thomas of Baxeby granted to Alan de Laton a toft and croft in the vill of Baxby and meadowland. John had been given this property by his father and it had belonged at one time to Thomas de Baxeby, deacon. Among the witnesses to his death was Steffan (Stephan) de Baxeby, brother of Geoffrey de Husthwaite, Dean of Bulmer. In the late thirteenth century Thomas the clerk, son of William de Baxeby, granted to his son John, in fee simple, the land tenements which he Thomas had of the gift of Robert Baxeby, once Lord of Baxby. The property included the right to have in meadows of Baxby three cows with their calves, twenty sheep with their lambs, a horse and a foal, and in the woods ten pigs without pannage, paying to the lord of Baxby half a pound of cummin at Easter and performing four perches of ''loning'' (possibly new cultivation) yearly. One of the witnesses was Robert de Baxeby, reeve.

Thomas of Middelton and Adam of Baxby conveyed a carucate at Baxby to Alan de Lek (Leake) in 1301. John Daiville - now of Egmanton - conveyed Thornton Manor and two mills in Baxby to John de Ellerker senior who was in possession until 1337. These mills then pass to the Sessay family and next to the Darells. There appears to be a third mill still in the Daiville family as, in 1391, William Daiville got permission from Byland to remove and rebuild the mill at Baxby. By now most of the land belonged to the Church of St. Peter in York or to Byland and Newburgh. The tithes of Baxby were released to William Baxby for ten shillings.

It is probable that William de Baxby, the son of William Wysbarn, was lord of Baxby and lived in the Manor House, when he was granted licences for an oratory in the years 1308 and 1314. In September 1316 William of Baxby was one of the purveyors appointed for Birdforth

Wapentake to raise supplies for the King's forces opposing the Scottish invasion. In 1327 there is a mention of William de Baxby, rector of Thormanby.

An atmosphere of fear and unrest prevailed caused by the Scotish invasions on one hand and dissatisfaction with the monarchy on the other. The able bodied men were constantly being called upon to fight, land was left uncultivated and harvests failed. The little that was left was commandeered by the King's army or stolen by the Scots. The taxable value of Baxby dropped from twenty nine shillings in 1301 to twelve shillings in 1322. Given these continuing conditions, plus the ravages of the Black Death in 1348 - 9, William Baxby must have found it extremely difficult to fulfill his appointment to provide supplies.

In 1357 we find one of the sheriff's deputies taking a bribe from William, son of Geoffrey Baxby, for not purveying hay or victuals from him. Master Robert Baxby, clerk, witnessed a deed of 8th August 1358 relating to land at Oulston. In 1392 the prebendary of Husthwaite complained that John de Baxby and others had broken his closes and hedges at Husthwaite, felled and carried away trees to the value of £100, assaulted his tenants and servants and threatened the Prebendary that for a long time he dared not leave his house. We know of Laurence Baxby in the years 1436-40. John Baxby in the years 1443-57, Alicia Baxby was also admitted as a member of the Corpus Christi religious order at York in 1453-4. John Baxby seems to have died about 1460 since letters of administration to his estate were granted on the 12 January 1461.

One of the most notable families in the fifteenth century was the Raggets. One was Henry who with John Cowper of Wildon led the first skirmish of the "Wars of the Roses" at Heworth in 1453. Agnes (wife of William) Ragget lived at Skawker (previously Skonoker), a substantial house within the township of Baxby before 1482.

After the Dissolution, the Baxby family collected the tithes, sublet from Trinity College. Records of 1539 - 40 state "Farm of tithes grain and hay in the vill and fields of Baxby - let to William Baxby for thirty six years at ten shillings." In the same year the Rectory of Coxwold was leased to

Richard Bellasis - "Tithe of hay, grain and wool in vills of Coxwold, Baxeby, Ulveston, Thornton and Angram."

In 1539 William Baxeby led men to a muster from Thornton cum Baxby. He is probably the William Baxbie of Baxby, gentleman who by his will dated 20th April 1556 directed that he should be buried in Coxwold Church. The last of the Baxbys recorded was Mistress Margaret Baxby in a will dated 1558.

The complexity of land ownership within the two manors of Husthwaite and Baxby is illustrated in a Tithe Cause document of 1557, which records a dispute between James Kytchingham of Carlton Husthwaite, husbandman and Margaret Baxby.

"Lands belonging to Husthwaite and Baxby doth lie in the fields called High Field where is lands of Prebend of Husthwaite and his tenants and also to lords of Baxby and their tenants belonging to the town of Baxby. The same was true of West Field, Acres Field and Arteby Field. Tenants of Husthwaite and Baxby haith bite of mouth together with their cattell in fields aforesaid and also in the commons called Husthwaite woods and commons. He hath seen the cellarer of Newburgh receive the privie tithe of the inhabitants of Baxby. Since the Dissolution. he hath heard Mr. Baxby took the privie tithes and tythe corn." Other inhabitants of Baxby in the sixteenth century include, George Bowerton, John Hunter, Rainold Atkinson and John Branton (labourer).

Chambers, Kitchinghams and Goultons.

John Chambers, Lord of the Manor of Baxby in the reign of Elizabeth I is thought to have married a Baxby and owned the whole manor by 1580 - 1. John died a freeman in 1606 and was succeeded by his son George who was buried at Coxwold in 1620. Arms were granted at a Yorkshire Visitation for a family named Baxbie, consisting of ermine two bars gules.

The muster records of 1569 for Birdforth Wapentake show the following as those who must provide armour, their ability to do so based on the value of their land and the richness of their wives' clothes. John Chambers of Baxby, John Burnett of Boscar and William Kitchinham at Carlton.

In the assessments for armour in 1580 just before the Armada, John Chambers is recorded as "a light horseman levied at forty shillings in Birdforth, and in the same year he voluntarily contributed in addition one petronell (pistol). Amongst those charged to carry private arms in 1613 were George Chambers of Thornton cum Baxby, Robert Kytchingham of Carlton and Richard Goulton of Byland.

Baxby Mills

The descent of Baxby Mills is incomplete. During the sixteenth century the Manor of Thornton was conveyed with three mills - one at Thornton and two at Baxby. They are mentioned in deeds of 1531 and 1581, then become separated from the manor when Sir Richard Cholmeley conveyed them to Roger Daiville. In 1612 Sir Roger Daiville and his wife Grace, conveyed them to Michael Askwith, gentleman.

In 1658, Christopher Goulton, a Baxby Yeoman, following a quarrel with John Myers, was charged with converting one of Baxby's water mills into a cottage without adding to it four acres of land according to the statute of Elizabeth 31.

Then in 1681 John Myers bought Red Keld Mill, There is a reason to believe that there was once a mill at, or close to, what is now Woolpots Farm. The present O.S. map shows a spring here named Red Keld. In 1818 a Manor Court Roll mentions grass at Red Keld Mill dam and race known as Short Acres. Baxby Mill was occupied before 1787 by John Asquith who died of consumption in that year. In 1816 it was occupied by Thomas Asquith.

Parish Registers

The parish registers of Coxwold name a number of persons living at Baxby in the seventeenth century, including George Chambers, gentleman, from 1621 until his death in 1640, and Edwin Sands Esquire (armiger) also in 1640. George Denham, the man hanged in York in 1664 for his part in the Farnley uprising was living at Baxby in the years 1655-8. Quarter Session records name Christopher Goulton of Baxby as one of the High Constables for Birdforth Wapentake from 1646-56. Edwin Sands above, was presented on 13th July, 1641, for encroachment on the highway from Baxby to Easingwold.

Also recorded in the Parish Registers were a number of Muncasters, Dorothy and John Bayleya, William and John Bartonne, Elizabeth and Robert Ward, Jacob and Edward Rimer, Willian and Allison Bel, John and Jane Barker and Jane and John Denham.

We know there were stocks at Baxby in 1610 since John Preston of Baxby was set in them for refusing to be a constable. In 1660 William Cass, wheelwright, refused to repair a hedge and ditch in Coxwold and part of the land between Crayke and Thirsk.

The manor of Baxby was also in the Newburgh estate for a few years having been purchased by Sir Thomas Bellasis from George Chambers. In 1641 however it was in the hands of the Sands or Sandys family and in 1659-60 Richard Sandys Esq. sold it to William Kitchingham Esq. of Toulston, near Tadcaster.

At that time the property consisted of a manor house and nine cottages. The manor seems to have passed by the marriage of Anne Kitchingham with Arthur Thornton. Arthur Thornton left it to his son, Sir William Thornton of York. Christopher Goulton of Highthorne, steward and legal agent for Lord Fauconberg, leased all the tithes of Husthwaite and Baxby for £20 in 1697. Baxby lands pass between the Kytchingham, Thornton and Goulton families. It was conveyed in 1789 by Col.Thornton to Thomas Plowman. Thomas Woodward of Aldwalk is said to have acquired it in 1791 and in 1890 his descendant John Woodward occupied the manor house, being in 1859 the property of John Dixon who lived at Throstle Nest, then a new house.

Baxby Manor House

The stone-built house has a south west facing main body, with a cross wing at the east end. On first sight the house would seem to be of eighteenth century date with Georgian windows, but research carried out by Barry Harrison since 1975 has revealed it to be of medieval origin. It is the only certain example of a base cruck/spere

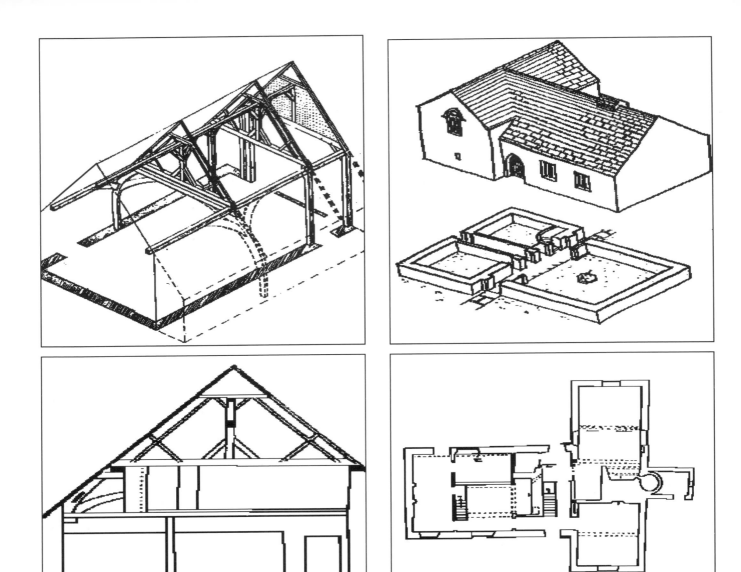

Plans of original Baxby Manor with base cruck construction pre-fourteenth century

truss structure in the north of England.

The main house body was a thirteenth century base-cruck aisled hall of two full bays with a high and low - or service - end, this latter possibly extending further west than at present; there is evidence of another truss in the gable end. The roof, now pantiled, has two massive crown posts, is heavily smoke encrusted and plastered between the rafters. The carpentry points to a pre-fourteenth century construction date.

Much of the original timber structure of the medieval hall is embedded in the stonework applied later (late seventeenth century or early eighteenth century) but the cruck-blade, aisle post and north wall plate can still be seen. We assume

that it was at this time that the aisle at the front on the house was removed, thus creating a two-storied elevation and that mullioned windows were put in - a remnant remains in the upper storey of the cross wing.

A huge bressumer had been inserted across the hall in the sixteenth century and it is upon this that the floor of the upper storey rests. The western end of the hall had a taking-in door to the upper storey and this may have been open to the roof until the early nineteenth century.

The present sixteenth century stone built cross wing at the east end replaced an earlier unit which extended into the area by at least one bay. Its size indicates that the wing would have been multi-functioned - a kitchen and unheated service room at the back, with a parlour at the front. A massive central stack serving both sides has a large bread oven which, unusually, projects outside, rather than into, an adjacent room.

Upstairs, there would be storerooms at the rear and a chamber at the front. A number of hearths were discovered during the renovation of the back rooms of the cross-wing, and the remnants of an early smoke hood are now visible in the hall beyond the bressumer.

That the house was quite grand when first built is illustrated by the style of construction and the decorative carving on the cruck blade and the aisle post. The site of medieval fish ponds behind the house also indicates the hall's status. It had its own Oratory in the fourteenth century - licences were granted to William de Baxeby in 1308 and 1314 - but its position is unknown. In 1605 it is described as a "capital messuage".

Unlike many manor houses, this one was never "Elizabethanised" or enlarged and improved to reflect the wealth and status of its owners. Rather they chose to live elsewhere and have it tenanted either by their own servants or let out as a farm.

The arrangement of space in the house has changed over the years as would be expected, but its evolution is not always clear. However, the will of George Chambers in 1620 and the inventory of William Frank, dated 13th October 1722, gives a clear indication of the number of rooms and their uses at these dates.

Extract from the Will of George Chambers 1620

Chamber over Hall called Oswald Chambers his chamber.

Chamber over my own parlour

The new chamber

My own parlour

The nurserie.

By this time the house was being used as a farm house. It was flanked on the west side by a substantial barn with a threshing floor (now grade II listed) and an "L" shaped range of buildings including a cart shed, cow house and various stables and loose boxes, all stone-built and giving on to a quadrangle that was later used as an open fold yard. Behind the house is a cobbled court yard with a central well. Amongst other buildings around this yard a pig sty with a stone chute for the kitchen and dairy waste remains. At the front of the house is a walled garden. At the time of the Frank inventory, this was an open cobbled yard with a walled garden on the east side and the farm yard to the west. The mounting block is still there as are the cobbles under the lawn!

The 1851 census shows that the house was divided into two dwellings. One family entered by the north door of the cross passage and used the two rooms in the cross wing north of the chimney stack. A staircase was inserted giving directly into one of the two bedrooms above. This was the home of Matthew Miller, a farm labourer born in South Otteringham, his wife Ann and their two children.

The rest of the house was occupied by William Mason described as a farm labourer and mana-ger/bailiff, his wife Mary, three children and also Robert Wood, servant and labourer, and Jane Pallister, house servant.

In the census of 1881, William, Mary and two of their children with a grand daughter lived in the main house. A widow, Elizabeth Harrison, and her servant, Maria Critcham, lived in the cross wing.

During the early 1900's the farm buildings were increased. A Dutch barn was built and the fold yard covered by a slate roof [with a pigeon loft incorporated in the gable end] by Slater's firm. A wash house, four goose houses, dog kennels and privies were built. These latter are two separate two holers built in stone either side of the ashpit and all covered under a slate roof. In the time of the present owner's grandparents, only ladies were allowed to use the privy having access from the front garden; the men used the one at the back. Now in 1990s both sexes use the same 'facilities', but with the benefit of running water, inside plumbing, and electricity. A vast difference in living standards in just the last hundred years in the life of a house which has accomodated progress for seven hundred years.

14

Birdforth

At the heart of the Birdforth Wapentake[1] ("Gerlestre" or Earl's Tree in Domesday Book) where there is easy access over well-drained land not only westwards into the Vale of York and northwards to Thirsk but also eastwards through the Coxwold- Gilling Gap into Ryedale, is the village of Birdforth. Today this is just a loose grouping of half a dozen dwellings with their church beside the ever busy A19. This was once the administrative centre and meeting place for Coxwoldshire and surrounding parishes. The church of St. Mary of Norman origin is now sadly closed. Many local residents, including the Rev. Gill and Mrs. Etson-Rowe, are buried in the church yard which is still peaceful despite the nearby traffic. The school

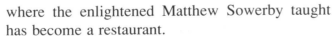
Burtree House. Site of Birdford Wapentake ('Gerlestre').

where the enlightened Matthew Sowerby taught has become a restaurant.

Birdforth Wapentake ('Gerlestre')

The realities which lie behind the name "gerlestre" are shrouded in the mists of antiquity but it may well be that the changing of the wapentake name to "Birdforth" has some significance and that it does not necessarily imply a change of venue. About half a mile upslope to the north side of Birdforth, and still within the township, there stands a long-established farmstead, now a racing stable, called "Burtree House". Students of place-names are well aware that a name often does not mean what it seems to do, so it is very unlikely that "Birdforth" has anything to do with birds or that "Burtree" has any connection with burs (or even with the "burtree, "bottry" or the elderberry). Bearing in mind the former importance of this locality it seems more likely that we have here the name element "burgh" (a mound, earthwork or small hill) [ref 1] which is of widespread occurrence in northern England and elsewhere. "Birdforth" would thus be the "ford near the burgh" and "Burtree House" would be named after a tree which was on or beside the "burgh". This tree, furthermore could be the "Earl's Tree" of pre-Domesday times. A glance down the list of Yorkshire wapentakes demonstrates how frequently there were named "howes" and "burghs": small hills, barfs or mounds, natural or artificial, were easily identifiable features of the landscape.

Another interesting point about Birdforth is that it is still shown as part of the ecclesiastical parish of Coxwold on nineteenth century maps. Clearly it was cut off from the main part of the parish when Carlton and Husthwaite were given to the

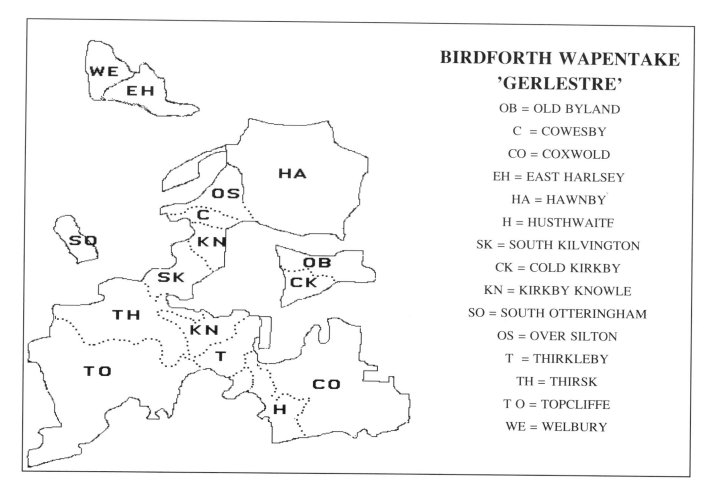

BIRDFORTH WAPENTAKE
'GERLESTRE'

OB = OLD BYLAND

C = COWESBY

CO = COXWOLD

EH = EAST HARLSEY

HA = HAWNBY

H = HUSTHWAITE

SK = SOUTH KILVINGTON

CK = COLD KIRKBY

KN = KIRKBY KNOWLE

SO = SOUTH OTTERINGHAM

OS = OVER SILTON

T = THIRKLEBY

TH = THIRSK

T O = TOPCLIFFE

WE = WELBURY

Archbishop by Ulfr just after the conquest (see Chapter 2) and, as prebend, led a separate existence from than onwards.

A19 and local routes north

The A19 which now plays such a central role in the existence of Birdforth is relatively recent. The Roman roads north did not use this route. In the twelfth century some roads were designated "Royal Routes" and had to be maintained to a minimum width. A local Royal Route was between York and Richmond crossing the Swale at Myton; there was an alternative Swale crossing at Thornton via Cundall and Asenby. Another Royal route north was from York by way of Crayke and Oldstead on into the Hambletons, later used by the Drovers and diverted through Bagby and Thirsk - contributing to the importance of the town.

A precursor of the A19 existed by the seventeenth century, passing through Easingwold. In 1749 a petition was presented to the House of Commons for a Turnpike between the short route between York and Northallerton. They noted that carriages could not pass in the winter though

some managed in the summer. The Act was initially rejected but passed in 1752.

It may interest the modern villager and road user to know that after Elizabethan times for many centuries it was the responsibility of the local inhabitants to maintain the roads with frequent fines for infringement.

Coal Mining at Birdforth

With regard to economic activity this locality remained predominantly agricultural, up to the eighteenth century when its history was punctuated by an unexpected phase of industrial development. Mining of Jurassic coal [3] in Coxwoldshire had certainly been carried on since the middle of the seventeenth century at Newburgh, Coxwold, Yearsley and elsewhere, but it is not until 1796 that we have any evidence of a number of pits on Lord Downe's land at "Birdforth Colliery" [ref 1].

The first mention of coal mining at Birdforth was in 1615 when a Mrs. Thornton owned a pit. In 1791 a colliery was started by John Horner which may have been based on Mrs. Thornton's workings.

The pit was later described as twelve yards deep and the coal seam in it was fourteen inches. John Horner was also involved with the lime pits at Kilburn which is where much of the Birdforth coal was used.

Prior to 1796 the mine was run by Luke Punshon and it was taken over by Lord Downe in that year. Between 1796 and 1798 it was run on his behalf by Luke Plummer, who was the "over-looker".

At any one time about thirty men were employed in the mine. "Hewers" who were also termed "Colliers" did the digging and were paid according to the amount of coal they brought out of the ground. "Drifters" drove the passages between various shafts to form access ways.

"Hurrying" was the dragging of loaded "corves", baskets, from the workplace to the shaft bottom and returning empty corves to the colliers.

As the Birdforth mine was situated more or less in a a small valley, one of the problems was the fact that all the water drained into the shafts from the surrounding land. To overcome this difficulty a pump was employed which was kept working night and day. It was driven by a steam engine - probably one of the first in the North Riding.

The ability of some colliers in hewing coal can be seen from the work sheets. The Hewers earned much more than the other employees. One hewer, William Foster, earned £1 18s 4d for hewing ten dozen and three corves (133), this was a very good week. During 1796 he was the highest wage earner but even his output dropped towards the year end. During the first months of 1797 he levelled off at thirteen corves a day. An entry for 28th April to 5th May states, "for some weeks past William Foster and William Stoney have filled thirteen corves each day as though limiting their output deliberately." This leads one to wonder if it could have been a reaction to jealousy by less able workmen.

New Year's Day 1798 proved disastrous for the Birdforth Colliery. We read, "The pit fell in...all the work force were engaged in trying to re-open the collapsed shaft". There is no further mention of coal output until January 8th and after January 26th all records of this nature ceased. By January 29th the colliery was closed.

In William Metcalfe's diary [2] we read for the above date, "The colliery at Burdforth given over, and the labourers paid off today at Jacky's (William Metcalfe's brother) it was begun by John Horner in the beginning of 1791"

References

[1] John S. Owen CTLSB, No 8, pp 1 - 12.

[2] William Metcalfe's Diary. Reprinted by Easingwold Advertiser.

[3] The material of Coal Mining at Birdforth was supplied by John Butler of Carlton Husthwaite.

---

¹WAPENTAKE

The term 'Wapentake' is derived from an old Scandanavian word meaning "weapon shake" referring to the symbolic flourishing of weapons to indicate agreements in the open air to public decisions. Wapentakes are found mainly in northern England with a strong Danish influence - elsewhere in the country the equivalent gathering was the 'hundred'. In time they became responsible for raising armies, raising taxes and law and order. They were the predecessors of Local Government and Parliament.

Gerlestre Wapentake (later Birdforth) was mentioned in Domesday when all its parishes were included except Hawnby and East Harlsey, which were with Allerton Wapentake. but by the end of the thirteenth century the wapentake was complete. Allerton and Birdforth wapentakes were closely associated and at one time contained the west riding parish of Feliskirk, including part of Kilburn.

Birdforth wapentake was held by the King throughout, though at times in the hand of the Lascelles and Dishforth familes.

15
Coxwold

Coxwold is one of the most beautiful villages in North Yorkshire. It is situated in the heart of Coxwoldshire on the old road between York and the north, at the western end of the Gilling Gap, a narrow valley linking the Vales of York and Pickering. For centuries it has been an agricultural community closely associated with the Bellasis family whose descendants, the Wombwells, still live at Newburgh Priory a mile to the south east. Plaques on many cottages bear the crest of Sir George Orby Wombwell and the date when each cottage was renovated. One of Coxwold's parsons, Laurence Sterne, brought the village world renown - he was an eccentric genius who amused his readers with two novels, "The Life & Opinions of Tristram Shandy, Gentleman" and "A Sentimental Journey".

Coxwold is an former market town with a charter dating back to 1304 granting a weekly market and Annual Fair to be held on the Assumption of the Blessed Virgin. The weekly market has long since disappeared but the Fair continues despite various lapses and is now held on the last week-end in June.

Today Coxwold is no longer remote and, apart from agriculture, its trade is now based on tourism. A successful pottery is run by Jill and Peter Dick and there is a furniture making enterprise.

Once an estate village owned by the Priory, now much of the property has been sold, but with covenants that seek to retain its architectural character. The outline of the village plan is very much the same as when it appeared on a map in 1605. Its houses (stonefaced in the nineteenth century by the then squire Sir George Orby Wombwell) with garths to the rear line the broad grass-banked street that climbs westwards to the church of St. Michael. Superficially it looks more like a Cotswold village than a North Riding hamlet. The ground plan of Coxwold is a simple rectangle with the church at the top of the hill and a line of cottages on either side with a cross roads at the bottom. It shows signs of having been a planned village which is not uncommon in this area. These villages are often associated with resettlement following a devastation but it is more likely to be the result in Coxwold of land management by one of its many estate owners.

Coxwold may have been an ancient 'estate centre' predating Roman times. It was probably the principal settlement with Baxby, Oulston, Birdforth and Thirkleby as outlying communities cleared in Galtres Forest.

The first written mention was during Anglo-Saxon times in a letter from the Pope in 757 to the King of Northumbria asking him to restore the monasteries at Stonegrave and 'Cuckawald'. The site of this early church is unknown but may have been on the site of Newburgh Priory.

Arms of Sir George Orby Wombwell on a Coxwold cottage

In Domesday Coxwold is called by its Saxon name *Cuckvalt*, or "Cuckoo Wood" (Cuc - to cry, valt - a wood). Centuries of erratic spelling have resulted in Cucvalt becoming *Cukewald* in the 13th c.; *Cuckold* in the 17th c.; *Coxwould* in the 18th c. - and finally Coxwold.

Before the Conquest, Coxwold belonged to the Earls of Northumbria and after William's victory passed to the Saxon Cofsi, one of Tostig's closest followers. He was granted, by royal charter, "soc and sac, toll and theam", - (the right to hold a manorial court, to be judge, and to receive fines and taxes). He did not hold it for long. After the Harrying of the North, Hugh Son of Baldric (Sheriff of York) was granted most of Coxwold-shire. He clearly concentrated much of the remaining population on his Coxwold estate since

although most of the surrounding manors are described as 'waste' in Domesday, Coxwold had appreciated from £6 to £12.

The Colvilles

After a complicated series of changes the manor was held by the Norman Colville family who as military subtenants of the Mowbrays also had land at Yearsley, Oulston and Melton Mowbray. They were to live in the area for over four hundred years. Colville Hall, a seventeenth century gabled and mullioned building next to the church is on the site of the first Manor House. The adjoining farm is still called Manor Farm.

About 1608, Colville Hall was bought by Sir Henry Bellasis of Newburgh who then became Lord of the Manor. He is probably responsible for the present facade. The Hall has an enormous fireplace with an external chimney breast which is similar to the one in Shandy Hall. Its other exceptional feature is a painted-glass window by Gyles of York, showing the arms of the Bellasis family with those of the families they had married into. The Hall was extended northwards in 1890 and has since been divided.

St. Michael's Church

A church at Coxwold was given to Newburgh by Roger de Mowbray with ten bovates of land. He also gave the monks chapels at Thirkleby, Kilburn and Over Stilton. Husthwaite church was also a chapel of Coxwold. The present building, with its octagonal west tower, battlements and pinnacles was built in the perpendicular style about 1450. For a small village church it is exceptionally large and contains some fine monuments, many of which relate to the Bellasis family.

On the north side of the chancel is the ornate monument of Sir William Bellasis (died 1603) and his wife Margaret Fairfax, he is lying ruffed in armour with his children kneeling below. The monument was originally brightly painted though now somewhat faded. ''Thomas Browne did carve this tombe. Himself alone of Hesselwood stone''. The next monument westwards is a pretentious group, attributed to Grinling Gibbons, portraying Henry Bellasis (died 1647) in Roman costume with a contemporary wig and his son Thomas (died 1700). Henry is holding a coronet while his son's manner seems to indicate he should disclaim it. On the opposite wall is Nicholas Stone's neo-classical monument of Thomas, 1st Viscount Fauconberg (died 1652) and his wife Barbara Cholmley. They kneel one behind the other with Thomas in a furred robe and Barbara in an elegant veiled gown and ruff. On the north wall of the nave is the sad memorial to the two sons of Sir George and Ladia Julia Wombwell who died in India and South Africa.

The wooden ceiling, with its decorative bosses, is the original one; it looks down on the nave with its 18th century two - decker pulpit (once it had three decks) and box-pews, some still with locks, put in to seat the large congregation that came to hear Coxwold's Laurence Sterne. On 25th September 1761, Richard Chapman, the estate agent, wrote to Lord Fauconberg of Newburgh Priory, 'Inclosed is a new plan for the pews in Coxwold Church which is a new Scheem of Mr. Sterne's...it will be Something in the form of a Cathedral, it will give a better Sound, a better light, and will all face the Parson alike, and the other way half the Church will be with their backs to the pulpit, which will make a Dispute for their seats.' It is possible that the curious tongue shaped communion rail was also designed by Sterne to allow more communicants access in the crowded chancel.

The Church has a Breeches Bible[1], a Register dating back to 1583, four little wooden mice carved by the Mouseman of Kilburn, the Hanoverian Royal Arms above the chancel arch, and Queen Mary's signature in the Visitor's Book; and so it is not only a beautiful place of worship but also a fascinating record of local history.

---

[1] A Breeches Bible is so- called because of the substitution of the word ''breeches'' for ''aprons'' in Genesis 3 v7.''Adam and Eve sewed themselves breeches''. It was printed in 1601 by Robert Barker, printer to Elizabeth 1 and more properly called the Geneva Bible.

Shandy Hall

Shandy Hall was an open hall, built c.1450 probably as a priest's house. Fragments of wall paintings still survive on an original wall. After the Reformation it became part of the Bellasis estate and it was added to in the seventeenth and eighteenth centuries. By then it was known as the Parsonage House. In 1696 a Mrs. Hartas was turned out of the house to accommodate the curate. She had let it fall into disrepair. Mr. Michael Fox spent fifteen days mending the house for Parson Brown to occupy. There is still a Fox family of builders in Husthwaite today.

It continued to be used as a Parsonage till 1807, then there was a succession of different tenants until, in 1966, the Laurence Sterne Trust was set up to restore the house. This with the aid of generous support and the energy of the Monkman family it was able to do. Decorating and gardening started in 1970 perhaps a continuation from September, 1760 when Sterne wrote ''...If you honour me with a Letter...it will find me either pruning, or digging, or trenching or weeding or hacking up old roots or wheeling away Rubbish...''

Sir John Harte, Lord Mayor of London

The Old Hall, almost opposite the church, was once the Free Grammar School of Coxwold endowed by Sir John Harte. Harte was a native of Kilburn who became apprenticed in London and married his master's daughter. He was very successful in business and became Sheriff of London in 1579 and Lord Mayor in 1589. He was knighted, became an MP and a founder Governor of the East India Company. He only had daughters who in turn married into wealthy families. With no sons and after providing for his daughters he left his money to a varied selection of charities. His legacies were huge. He was much wealthier than the Bellasis, his grandchildren received sums ranging from £100 to £333. The misterie of Grocers Company were given a revolving loan of £100 to set young men up in business and two great livery pots each weighing ninty seven ounces. There were gifts to Christs Hospital, St. Thomas' and Bethlem, prisoners, the relief of the poor debtors and to the marriage of 60 poor maid servants with £30 10s each. He left £10 to the poor of Coxwold and £6 13s 4d to

The old Grammar School at Coxwold. Founded by Sir John Harte.

Kilburn and Helmsley. Most importantly he left the manor of Nether Silton to his son in law if he and his heirs paid the free school £36 13s 4d a year and further sums to maintain the schoolmaster and his staff.

He made Sidney Sussex College, Cambridge, responsible for visiting the school and for this were to get 20s a year for a feast. Unfortunately Cambridge is a long way from Coxwold and there is no record that anyone made the journey - rather remiss of them as he also left other large sums to the college for Exhibitions, Fellow's salaries and the library.

The front page ''The York Courant'' Sept. 1761 advertised 'The Noted School of Coxwold. Fourteen Guineas a - year for Board and Lodging, By the Rev. Thomas Newton, B.A. and Assistants. All imaginable Care will be taken to cultivate and adorn boys' tender Minds to enable them to fill the several Stations of Life they are designed for, as become Men, and Christians.' The school was sold in 1894, since when it has been a private house, for many years occupied by Mr. Giepel.

SIR JOHN HARTE KNIGHT SOMETIME CITIZEN &Lo. MAYOR OF Ye CITY OF LONDON CAUSED THIS SCHOOL TO BEE ERECTED AT HIS OWNE COSTE AND CHARG^S, WHERIN HE PROVIDED COMPLETE MAINTENANCE AND STIPEND FOR ONE SCHOOLE M^R AND ONE USHER AND ALSO 4 MARKS YEARLY TO A PETTY USHER TO TEACH YOUNGE CHILDREN IN THIS TOWNE^S AND 20 FOR 3 SERMONS TO BE PREACHED AT THIS CHURCHE. HE ALSO BESTOWED ON SIDNEY COLLEGE IN THE UNIVSITY OF CAMBRIDGE 4 SHOLLERSHIPS AND TWO FELLOWSHIPS FOR SCHOLLERS COMING FROM THIS SCHOLE AND MOREOVER A GREEKE LECTURE AND 30£ TOWARDE YE FURNISHING OF THEIR LIBRARY TOGITHER WITH A STIPEND UNTO YE M OF TE SAIDE colledge. Towards ye bulidinge of this schoole ye right hoable ye Edwarde Wotton bestowed most pte of ye stones wf slate & 12 timber trees out of his Manor of Bylande & hath allowed to ye schoole in turfes for fire.

The Fauconberg Arms

The Fauconberg Arms was the Belasyse Arms until 1823. Then the publican was a William Barwick; the inn was handed on from father to son, as the publican back in 1768 had also been a Barwick and at the sale after Sterne's death he bought a little table that can be seen at Shandy Hall. The Prison House is thought to date from the eighteenth century. It was used as the overnight lock up for drunks. It is very conveniently situated next to the pub! It is not known when it was last used as a jail and is now a dwelling house.

The Almshouses, originally called the Poor Men's Hospital, was founded in 1662, by

Thomas Earl Fauconberg. He provided an endowment of £59 annually, available to ten alms-people. It now houses six in greater comfort! It is thought that the central portion with the belfry, called the Bell-house, was originally intended as a chapel for the alms-people In the early nineteenth century, the Bell-house was occupied by the usher from the Grammar School. Here he taught the younger children to read as they sat on long forms.

In the summer of 1761, Sterne visited a dying widow, possibly at the almshouses. He administered the sacrament, then he asked the woman what she would bequeath him. Her reply was that she had nothing, not even for relations. Sterne answered, "That excuse shall not serve me. I insist upon inheriting your two children.". He became their benefactor.

The Almshouses were restored and modernised inside, in 1962 by Capt. and Mrs. V.M. Wombwell - with the help of a grant from the Pilgrim Trust. "Senior citizens", who pay rent live in them now.

Thirsk to Malton Railway (The T and M)

In 1853 a railway line was opened from Pilmoor Junction on the Thirsk to York route passing through Coxwoldshire to Malton.[1] This provided important communications and opportunities for this quiet backwater of the old North Riding. The line named the Thirsk and Malton (the T and M) existed for about 111 years and it can be said that the railway and its characters embodied a romance and folklore remembered vividly by those who knew and used it.

In the 1840s there had been a steady increase in the number of railway lines in the north of England accompanied by a complex series of mergers by smaller companies. The Great North of England Railway (the GNE) had opened the lines between York and Darlington in 1841 but was unable to extend to Newcastle. It was taken over by the Newcastle and Darlington Junction Railway (N and DJ) who completed the link between Darlington and Newcastle by 1844. The York and North Midland devloped the approaches from the south and opened the York Scarborough branch in 1845. By 1846 the GNE

merged with the NDJ to form the York and Newcastle Railway (Y&N) and the following year again merged with the Newcastle and Berwick Railway to form the York, Newcastle and Berwick Railway (the YNB). The Thirsk Malton line was planned in turn by three companies, the N&DJ, the Y&N and YNB.

At Coxwold Station one of only two passing hoops was situated (the T and M being a single track line). From 1895 annual competitions for the best kept stations were held and Coxwold was a regular "First Prize Winner". Facilities at Coxwold included the passing loop, a signal box, horse dock, cattle dock, weigh office, two platforms and two waiting rooms (one first class, carpeted and the walls hung with prints of the Wombwell family from nearby Newburgh Priory). In its heyday Coxwold boasted gravel platform surfaces.

The railway was used by freight and passenger trains. Military personnel and vehicles were carried in both world wars. During the second war both the King and Winston Churchill travelled along the line. The second world war left its mark on the railway. Just west of Husthwaite Gate an almost empty train was machine-gunned by a Nazi fighter. Tom Inman, a signalman travelling to Sunbeck was unfortunately killed in this attack of 4th March 1945.

In another incident to the east of Coxwold a bomb jettisoned from a German bomber made a crater on the line. This failed to break the signal equipment and an early morning passenger train on its way to York ran directly into the crater. Fortunately no one was injured and amazingly no one heard the bomb blast in the night of the 26th July 1943.

On the 31st January 1953 the last scheduled passenger service ended on the T and M line. The last passenger train to stop at Husthwaite gate was a special excursion to Scarborough on 28th June 1962. The station at Coxwold closed to passengers on 1st October 1963 when another excursion train ran. Both Husthwaite and Coxwold closed to goods traffic on 7th August 1964.

[1] Howlat Patrick, "The Railways of Ryedale".

16
Newburgh and the Bellasis Family

A mile south east of Coxwold is Newburgh, the "novo burgh" of the Augustinian Canons who founded the priory here on land given by Roger de Mowbray after their journey from Bridlington and Hood (See Chapter 4). Today the village is merely a small collection of picturesque houses beside the road from Coxwold to Crayke. The dominating feature is Newburgh Priory with its associated lake, park and estate farms. This peaceful place has been associated with much English history.

This little route was once a great northern artery running from York up over bleak Black Hambleton to Durham and Scotland. It was used by King John and Henry III and the tragic Queen Margaret of Scotland. The Drovers used it to drive Galloway cattle to the markets of East Anglia and at the time of the Dissolution there were three or four coaching inns at Newburgh.

A great medieval writer, William de Newburgh, wrote his account of English history here in the thirteenth century; later Oliver Cromwell's daughter was to marry into the Bellasis family and (probably) bring his body to be buried at Newburgh. A Wombwell was to survive the Charge of the Light Brigade.

William de Newburgh

William de Newburgh was born in 1136 near Bridlington where at the age of ten he became a choirboy in the Priory. As a youth he kept notes on events in England and abroad. After an illness prevented him from taking part in normal monastic work he was persuaded by Ernald, abbot of Rievaulx, to write an account of his time. Thus began "Historia Rerum Anglicarum"

(A History of English Affairs), a plain account laced with tales of the supernatural. From the mouths of those present William recounts the events surrounding the death of Becket in Canterbury and from Mowbray's men of the second crusade of 1147. During 1192 a particularly exuberant display of the Northern Lights, such that the canons thought the monastery was on fire, heralded the capture of Richard II by the Duke of Austria - his ransom was to cost a year's wool from Newburgh.

For all his global view of events William never left the locality, except a visit to the hermit Godric who lived on the Wear. The History ends with his death in 1197 and he is presumed to have been buried in the monk's cemetery at Newburgh, now under the cricket pitch.

The Priory

The Augustinian Priory was built by the Canons between about 1145 and 1150. It was not as large as Byland or Rievaulx with some fifteen to twenty monks, but at the time of the Dissolution it was wealthier than either.

The grant appears to have given them all the land to the east of Coxwold. In effect, from the fishpond up along Long Beck, then across to the Holbeck - an area of flat known as Whiteacres - then down the gill to the East of the Park House and west along Malton Street to Husthwaite and Newburgh.

Little of the original priory building survives and nothing is known of its original layout. A massive chimney stack in the old kitchen court is all that survives. Even the church has disappeared.

Newburgh from the west through the gates said by Pevsner to be among the best in England

After the Priory was acquired by the Bellasis family at the Dissolution subsequent generations rebuilt and embellished the property turning it into a fine country house with parkland and extensive local estates. Much of the original house was built by Sir Henry Bellasis and it was extensively remodelled by the 4th Viscount in the eighteenth century. For fifty years he sought to turn a miscellany of buildings into a classical Georgian country house, though the result could never be a symmetrical whole due to the limitations of the original.

Since then two long ownerships have added to the house and saved it from destruction. Sir George, the 4th Baronet, modernised the estate and Captain Wombwell, with his wife Beryl, was able to restore much of the property after the war. The Priory is now the home of Sir George and Lady Wombwell, the heirs of the Bellasis family.

The house today is a large irregular building entered from the west through a fine wrought iron gate off the York-Coxwold road. The original building faced north and the central porch on the north is still there with a range to the right. On the left of the porch is the great hall that is a now a dining room. The old gallery is left as a ruin, the cost of restoring it was prohibitive, so the roof timbers were removed to make it safe.

The Bellasis Family

The founder of the House of Belasyse was a knight from Normandy who it is said defeated the Earl of Morcar and Hereford the Wake at Ely. In return for this favour William the Conqueror gave the family a huge tract of land to the north of the Tees. For many years their home was at Bellasis Hall near Billingham. In the fourteenth century John Bellasis to raise money for a crusade exchanged his estate for another, at Henknoll near Auckland, that was of poorer agricultural value. Any decrease in family fortune was, however, to be repaired by the somewhat sinister brothers Richard and Anthony who respectively obtained Jervaulx Abbey and New-burgh Priory in the aftermath of the Dissolution. Richard, a member of the Council of the North, removed the lead from Jervaulx in 1537 and with his brother dissolved some nine monasteries.

Anthony, a chaplain to Henry VIII, was able to obtain the Priory for £1062 14s. 2d. in June 1539. Henry VIII, who had been angered by the role played by some northern monasteries in the Pilgrimage of Grace, led by the Archbishop of York, allowed Thomas Cromwell to act as his agent for their disposal. Anthony was well placed to make a successful bid, which was allowed after the Prior had been tried by the Council of the North for allegedly criticising the King; he

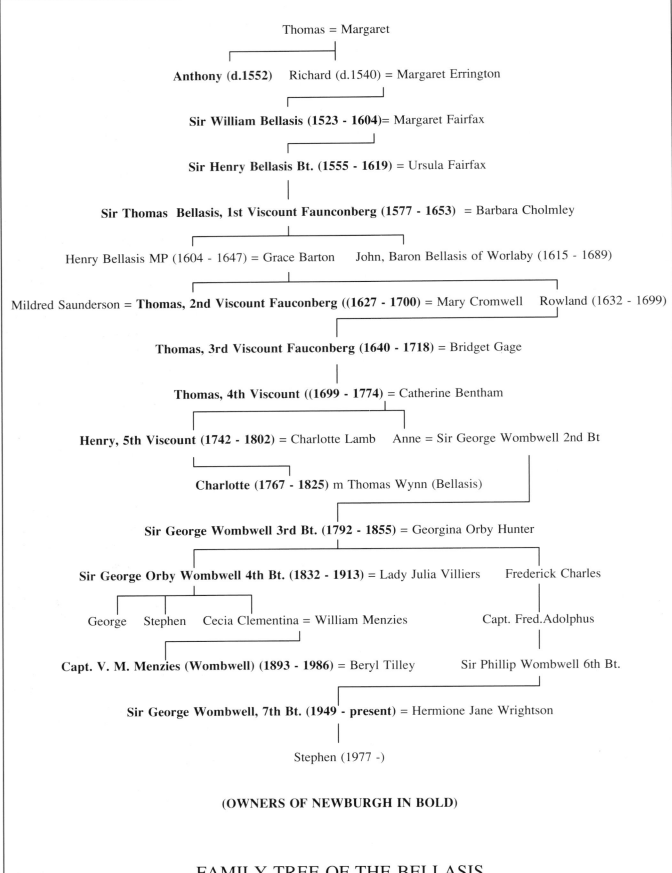

Thomas = Margaret

Anthony (d.1552)   Richard (d.1540) = Margaret Errington

Sir William Bellasis (1523 - 1604)= Margaret Fairfax

Sir Henry Bellasis Bt. (1555 - 1619) = Ursula Fairfax

Sir Thomas Bellasis, 1st Viscount Faunconberg (1577 - 1653) = Barbara Cholmley

Henry Bellasis MP (1604 - 1647) = Grace Barton   John, Baron Bellasis of Worlaby (1615 - 1689)

Mildred Saunderson = **Thomas, 2nd Viscount Fauconberg ((1627 - 1700)** = Mary Cromwell   Rowland (1632 - 1699)

Thomas, 3rd Viscount Fauconberg (1640 - 1718) = Bridget Gage

Thomas, 4th Viscount ((1699 - 1774) = Catherine Bentham

Henry, 5th Viscount (1742 - 1802) = Charlotte Lamb   Anne = Sir George Wombwell 2nd Bt

Charlotte (1767 - 1825) m Thomas Wynn (Bellasis)

Sir George Wombwell 3rd Bt. (1792 - 1855) = Georgina Orby Hunter

Sir George Orby Wombwell 4th Bt. (1832 - 1913) = Lady Julia Villiers   Frederick Charles

George   Stephen   Cecia Clementina = William Menzies   Capt. Fred.Adolphus

Capt. V. M. Menzies (Wombwell) (1893 - 1986) = Beryl Tilley   Sir Phillip Wombwell 6th Bt.

Sir George Wombwell, 7th Bt. (1949 - present) = Hermione Jane Wrightson

Stephen (1977 -)

(OWNERS OF NEWBURGH IN BOLD)

FAMILY TREE OF THE BELLASIS
AND WOMBWELL FAMILIES

died while "in ward" at Pomfret. Anthony was a "wary and prudent" man. Cromwell was executed for arranging the marriage between Henry and Anne of Cleves; Anthony signed the decree invalidating it and was rewarded to become a Prebend of Westminster.

Richard died in 1540 leaving his son William still a minor. When he came of age in 1552 among other properties he received the grant of Newburgh from Anthony, who was to die childless later that year.

William, who married Margaret, the strongly Roman Catholic daughter of Sir Nicholas Fairfax of Gilling Castle, spent much of his early years converting the monastic property of Newburgh into a manor house and establishing the family's hold on the estate. William was a prudent man who though born a Catholic, steered clear of the rising of the northern earls in 1569 and became High Sheriff of the North Riding in 1573.

Aveling says the Bellasis record on religion is dubious, the head of the family tending to move backwards and forwards between Catholicism and the Church of England with events, while the wives and younger sons remained loyal to Rome.

William was one of the four richest men in the county and added the manors of Yearsley and Old Byland with part of Coxwold to the estate. In 1554 he was knighted by Queen Mary and King Phillip. In Newburgh Priory two fine portraits of him can be seen; one as a young man shows him sharp eyed, red haired and vigorous. In 1604 he died and Henry, the eldest of his six sons, erected a fine monument to him in Coxwold Church of stone quarried from Hazelwood - later to supply York Minster.

William's son, **Sir Henry,** continued to embellish Newburgh, installing in the dining room the magnificent marble fireplace that was carved by Nicholas Stone. He also further enlarged the estate with the acquisition of Thornton-on-the-Hill and the rest of Coxwold. When he died in 1619, a colourful monument by Stone was placed in York Minster.

Thomas who succeeded him at the age of forty seven was MP for Thirsk and created **1st Viscount Fauconberg**. He married Barbara,

daughter of Sir Henry Cholmondeley of Brandsby, and together they produced two sons and five daughters. This pious Catholic family was to become an enemy of Lord Wentworth, Lord President of the Council of the North, resisting the payment of fines for not attending Anglican services. Quarrels with the Council resulted in the Viscount serving three months in Fleet Prison and passions only cooled when Wentworth was transferred to Ireland.

During the Civil War the Bellasis family played a prominent role on the Royalist side. Henry and his brother John with other leading families of the area - the Slingbys, Vavasours and Ingrams who were all related by marriage - raised regiments and served under the Marquis of Newcastle. After defeat at Marsden Moor Fauconberg and Vavasour fled to the continent but John joined the King at Oxford and was created Baron Belasyse of Worlaby. Towards the end of his life he was appointed Governor of Tangier that had come to Britain as part of the dowry of Catherine Braganza on her marriage to Charles II. While there in 1667 he learnt that his extravagant son Sir Harry had died in a drunken duel.

Henry's son **Thomas, the 2nd Viscount Fauconberg**, in a second marriage married Cromwell's daughter, Mary, at Hampton Court in a grand ceremony that lasted a week. The Protector gave her a dowry of £15000. After Cromwell's exhumation it is said Mary had her father's body brought to Newburgh and reinterred on the upper floor. Thomas was a courtly man appointed by Charles II as Ambassador to Venice and Italy. He was financially astute and in 1700 he left an estate valued at £6000 a year. Having no male heir the title passed to his nephew, again called Thomas. He was a quarrelsome man who went bankrupt before fleeing to a Convent in Brussels where he died in 1718.

His son, another **Thomas, the 4th Viscount Fauconberg**, after marrying Catherine, the daughter of a rich landowner, was able to restore the family fortune. During a long life he set about converting Newburgh into an elegant country house, though sadly for him he spent much time at their London home in George Street which his wife preferred to Newburgh.

His first rebuilding was the handsome stable block which may have been influenced by James Gibbs and Williams Wakefield. Subsequent development of the western part of the priory that gave the house a fine approach showed great skill but in the Yorkshire amateur spirit no architect was formally engaged. The Newburgh accounts give the names of many craftsmen; Daniel Harvey, carver; Edward Mortimer, glazier; Charles Mitley, carver; and importantly Cortese, a skilled Italian plasterer who worked in many Yorkshire houses.

Bellasis. Argent a chevron gules between three fleurs de lis azure.

"Bonne et Belle Assez"

Thomas not only transformed the priory but also did immense work on the gardens and old deer park - for many years spending £500 per annum.

Thomas died in 1774 and was succeeded by **Henry** who married Charlotte Lamb, sister of Lord Melbourne. He became the MP for Peterborough and Lord of the Bedchamber to George III. They had four daughters but no son. Consequently Newburgh was inherited by the eldest daughter **Charlotte** who married Thomas Wynn. They lived mainly in London.

The **Wynn-Belasyses** had no children and on Charlotte's death the estate passed through her sister Anne who had married **Sir George Wombwell** of Stowlangtoft - though he kept a large racing stable at Manor Farm, Byland. George served with the 10th Hussars under Wellington in Spain during the Peninsular Wars and was a close friend of George IVth. Poodle Wombwell was said to be the only friend of the king "whom the example and companionship of

that monarch did not bring ruin''. His lofty approach to life did not extend to maintaining Newburgh so that on his death the house and estate had suffered considerable neglect.

Their son **George, 3rd Baronet,** inherited on the death of Charlotte and married Georgina Orby Hunter of Lincolnshire in June 1824. The Wombwells again spent much of their time in London where a son, **George Orby**, was born in 1832. At the age of eighteen he joined the 17th Lancers and was sent to the Crimea as an aide to Lord Cardigan where he survived the Charge of the Light Brigade...though his horse was killed under him. A picture of his favourite horse, The Turk, which survived the Crimean War can be seen at the house. Its gravestone is in the Long Gallery.

Old Sir George had died unexpectedly in January 1855 leaving the estates and coal mines in Cheshire to his younger sons requiring George Orby to concentrate on renewing Newburgh with reduced funds.

This he did with energy using steam ploughs to bring the deer park under cultivation and the introduction of many modern farming techniques. He married Lady Julia Villiers the daughter of the 6th Earl of Jersey. The estate was 12000 acres and he did much to encourage an agricultural revolution among his tenants. George and Julia had three daughters and two sons. Tragically young George died of Typhoid in India and similarly his brother Stephen in South Africa, where he was serving in the Boer war. In 1874 the Prince of Wales came to Newburgh for an elaborate partridge shoot. He arrived at Coxwold via York station where only "the better dressed" were allowed in. George Orby lived to an old age and died in 1913. In 1901 it was said "no one seeing him ride a spirited thorough-bred through the Park, or drive a dashing pair of horses down Picadilly would believe that he took part in the Balaclava charge and was born in the early 1830s''.

He was succeeded after the death of Lady Julia in 1921 by **Captain Malcolm Menzies** (Wombwell), on condition he changed his name to Wombwell. His father had married Sir George's youngest daughter Cecilia. Captain Wombwell who married Beryl Tilley served with the Royal

Scots in their retreat from Mons during the first World War and with the Scots Guards at Ypres and Passchendale. At the outbreak of the Second World War thinking he would not be able to live there again, he leased Newburgh to a boys school for twenty one years. Fortunately the school left early and with help from the Historic Buildings Council and plans from Sir Martyn Beckett, work to restore the property began in 1960 not before it had been extensively damaged by fire. Captain and Mrs. Wombwell provided the energy and enthusiasm to undertake one of the finest restorations of the post-war period.

There were no children of the marriage to Beryl Tilley and on his death the estates passed to **Sir George Wombwell the 7th Baronet** who inherited through Frederick the youngest son of Sir George and Lady Georgina. In 1977 **Stephen Wombwell** was born.

The Park and Garden

The park at Newburgh was originally a medieval deer park. These were usually made using high artificial fences to retain deer within a confined area of ancient woodland. They were costly to construct and maintain. They had to be large enough for the chase but also the timber products were an important part of the estate revenue - providing steady income from regular felling or a large sum if the owners needed rapid access to capital.

A 1605 survey of Newburgh when the main entrance to the house was on the north side shows a formal walled garden laid out as a number of square parterres to south. Beyond was an enclosed deer park extending beyond to the south east with farm land between. This was probably laid out by William Bellasis, nephew of the founder.

A survey of 1722 shows that little had changed except that the park had been enlarged and a small hill to the south known as the Mount had been planted. But by 1744 all was different. The house was approached from the west, the old entrance courtyards on the north had been removed and a small lake created, fed by an aqueduct from Byland. On the south side the formal garden had been replaced by a sweeping lawn with a pleasure Garden containing a bowling green and thatched tennis court to the south east of the house. This work was undertaken by the 4th Viscount who spent prodigious sums on the garden and planting avenues of trees in the park. The extent of this was sufficient to require the establishment of a tree nursery. The "Stripe" along the road to Oulston was planted in 1723. The long enclosing park wall was built at this time and the Newburgh archives record paying Michael Fox for this work. All of this happened before Capability Brown and there is no known designer though it is suggested that Stephen Switzer who worked at Castle Howard was influential. The garden continued to develop and was added to by Sir George Orby and more recently Captain Wombwell.

Wombwell. Gules a bend between six unicorns' heads razed argent.

"In well Beware".

Sources:

(1) In Well Beware, G.R.Smith.
(2) Newburgh Priory. John Cornforth. Country Life, March 1974.
(3) Planting for Pleasure and Profit. Giles Worsley. Country Life, November 1988.
(4) Topiary, Royalty and Wild Waters. Ken Lemmon. Country Life, April 1986
(5) Newburgh Archives. NRYCC Record office.

The House and Gardens are open to the public on Wednesday and Sunday afternoons in the season.

17

Husthwaite

S. Barker   B. Duffield R. S. Eyre   D.Wilkinson

Husthwaite lies in the south west corner of Coxwoldshire about 200 feet above sea level on undulating countryside that is elevated to the north east where the Howardian Hills end and an old beacon was situated on the ridge. As in the past it is predominaantly an agricultural village growing cereals, potatoes and oilseed rape with sheep and cattle rearing. Unlike Coxwold it has little modern tourism but is becoming a commuter and retirement home for nearby towns. It has a successful bus company and a few high tech residents who conduct their business through computer linked telephones. There are still in Husthwaite many residents whose families have lived in the area for generations.

Husthwaite village has a long main street running east to west with St. Nicholas' church at the mid point where a road, known as the Nooking, branches off to Easingwold. It lies north of Malton Street which was probably part of a Brigantean tract and later a Roman road from Malton (Derventio) to Aldborough (Isurium of the Brigantes). On the outskirts of the village to the west is a charming old house known as Highthorne with commanding views over the Vale of York, now occupied by the Cameron family.

Parallel to the old Thirsk to Malton railway track is Elphin beck that drains much of the northern Parish and flows into the Swale while the southern area is drained by the River Kyle that flows into the Foss.

Husthwaite is a "new" village; it was not mentioned in Domesday when it was part of Baxby - now only a few houses on the edge of Husthwaite. The name means "the clearing in a wood with a house in it". Several Roman coins covering the reigns of emperors down to Honorius are said to have been found on the side of the track leading to Flower o' May farm. From the reign of Henry II to about 1228 Husthwaite was in the Forest of Galtres but was 'ridden out' in 1217; it remained in the purloin for forest purposes probably until the early eighteenth century.

Origin and Growth

There are no known documents and there is no direct archaeological evidence for the way in which early Husthwaite grew, or for the location of its earliest beginnings (Chap 2.) Nevertheless the form of the village plan suggests that the original settlement ran southwards from the present church and green towards Malton Street, along the line of the Easingwold Road, now called The Nooking. If this was the original village street, it seems to have narrowed as it left the village green and funnelled out again onto what appears to have been a common on the steep hillside to the east. This is all shown on section A of the extract of the 1841 tithe map. The simple plan of this small central section is quite different from the sections to the east and west along the present main street. These have long curving garths running back behind each of the individual holdings, and their reversed-S shape shows clearly that they were carved out from the pre- existing sections of the open fields of the township. In other words there was a functioning settlement here before these parts of it (B, and C on the map) were built upon. Details of the ground plan suggest that the messuages of the western part of the village were sited along the headlands of two former furlongs (Band C)

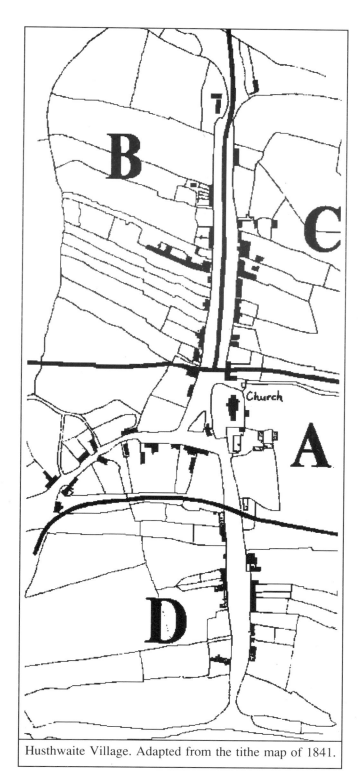

Husthwaite Village. Adapted from the tithe map of 1841.

lands being appropriated would be common open field subject to co-operational arrangements. Such changes would require complicated agreements within the manor. One possibility is that these developments took place during the century or two following the harrying of the north when population re-expanded to re-occupy land which, as noted in Domesday Book had been "waste" in 1086 [refs 1,2].

The Prebend

Husthwaite Manor appears to have been given by its ancient owner, Ulfr, to the Minster at about the time of the Norman Conquest. The village from that time belonged to the church and not a local resident lord of the manor - which probably gave it a more independent spirit than neighbouring villages. The Archbishops appointed a prebendary as lord of the manor but this was usually leased to provide rental income. There is still a prebendary canon of Husthwaite with a stall in York Minster but the Ecclesiastical Commissioners sold the property in 1853 to John Dixon of Throstle Nest near Baxby, lord of the manor of Husthwaite in 1853-9. It then came to William Harrison and later to Edward Harrison who died in 1911.

The Church

There was a chapel at Husthwaite in which Newburgh Priory had a resident priest from the end of the twelfth century. The mother church was Coxwold and in 1546 it was granted with the church at Coxwold to Trinity College, Cambridge, that held the advowson till 1864. In the eighteenth and early nineteenth centuries they were leased to the Fauconbergs.

The parish church dedicated to St. Nicholas is an attractive original twelfth century building that retains much of its Norman architecture. Over the years it has been adapted and re-styled. The west tower was built in the fifteenth century, possibly following a border raid when church towers were used as strongholds.

On entering through a modern porch (the date 1878 is carved above the entrance) there is the original archway built about 1140. It is low and massive with typical order columns, spiral capitals and zigzag ornamentation. Porches had many

while the eastern section (D) was made out of one furlong by cutting the main street across the middle of it. It will be seen that the strip length within all three of the postulated furlongs approximates to 220 yards (ten chains or one furlong).

Whether the expansion took place in one phase or in several cannot even be guessed at. It seems unlikely that it could have occurred in an unordered or random fashion, however, since the

Husthwaite Church before the war memorial was built and with the old house on the Green,.

uses; they were shelter for the night watchman, a school and a place where the priest prepared the children for confirmation. Through the ancient oak door below the arch is the nave with the chancel beyond, both with original walls. Opposite the main entrance stands a doorway now filled in.

The windows on the northern side of the nave are of Norman construction but those on the south date from 1895. Straight headed box pews on either side were installed in the seventeenth century, before this there were no pews at all. The massive roof timbers are the work of Robert Thompson, the woodcarver from Kilburn, when re-roofing of the nave and tower were carried out in 1907-9. In 1935 he carved the altar table and reredos. The mouse emblem can be seen on all his work.

At the western end stands a fairly modern font with a seventeenth century wooden cover. Looking eastward is the altar with beautiful stained glass above. To the left of the chancel arch there is a small window known as a hagioscope or squint that enabled the worshippers to observe the priest at the altar. The pulpit has a canopy and an open work ogee cupola similar to the font cover. Attached to the back of the pulpit is a lead crucifix, an example of a fourteenth century coffin cross found in the churchyard in the 1930s.

Several memorials are placed on the walls to the memory of local clergy. The Rev. John Winter who was curate of the parish for nearly sixty five years, the Rev. Robert Peirson Archdeacon of Cleveland and minister of the parish, and the Rev. T. Midgely headmaster of Coxwold School for fifty three years who died in 1761. Beneath the east end of the church is the family vault of the Goultons, a family whose ancestors fought at Hastings and for many years lived at Highthorne.

On the south side of the chancel is a piscina (a wash basin); this is a fifteenth century replica of a Saxon original. The tower of the church holds three bells, now "dead hung" since restoration in 1960, whose dates and inscriptions are; Treble, 1707, "O come let us sing unto the Lord"; Second, 1621, "Jesus be our speed"; Tenor, 1726, "The death I bewail, the people I call". The tenor bell was cast by Edward Seller of York and inscribed with the names of the church wardens - John Sharrow, John Wailes and William Barker.

The church organ dated 1920 was not new when installed. It was said to have been positioned too near the font as it restricted people from standing around it at a christening. Now in 1990 it has been overhauled. The name plate shows its builder to be T. Wadsworth of Huddersfield.

A restoration was carried out in 1907-8 when the chancel, nave and tower were re-roofed and the south-west corner of the nave rebuilt. The parish registers survive from 1674. A record was kept for a time of burials according to the Act for burying in woollen only. Thus on 3rd October

1678 Robert Husthwaite was buried without a coffin wrapped only in sheep's wool.

In 1856 the curacies of Husthwaite and Birdforth were united and in 1864 the Ecclesiastical Commissioners with the consent of Trinity College transferred the patronage of Husthwaite to the Archbishop of York who was already patron of Birdforth. In 1897 the church yard was supplemented by the formation of a new cemetery controlled by the parish council, this being a portion of field offered by James Wilson of Highthorne. There is no longer a vicarage in Husthwaite. The house built in 1908 is now a private house. The last vicar to reside there was Rev. Tyler.

Husthwaite is said to have been one of the first places in the area visited by the early Methodist preachers and in 1797 it was regarded as a Methodist village. When the Easingwold Circuit was formed in 1800 there were however only five or six members of the Husthwaite society. There were eight in 1814, namely Francis Tesseyman, John and Ann Wragg, Ann Sheperd, Betty and Francis Batty, Elizabeth Warin and Jane Yallow. A methodist chapel was built in 1841.

Reverend and Mrs. John Winter. Vicar 1809 - 1873.

The 19th Century. Mr. Taylor's [1] Account.

On Gibbet Hill a post stood where Mr. Rudd's cottage is, on which people who had done wrong were hung up and gibbeted. Lists field where Beacon Banks now stands was a bare field. At every road gates marked the boundaries and there were no gardens. Most people kept geese and a few ewes.

I have seen Acaster Hill, Red House. Throstle Nest and Woolpots ... as old thatched houses and taken tea at the big clippings parties that used to be given every year.

A Quarry was in Mr. Slater's garden, where stone was got to mend the roads. Blocks of stone were got out of a field near Highthorne to help make the railway and prop the blocks of wood. There were no closing times at the public houses, and when the railway was being built the navvies drank all night and slept anywhere. I was one of the first to ride on the train when the line was open and the carriages were open at the top. The line was from Raskelf to Pickering.

When there was a wedding the boys had to race to the brides house, and the first there got a piece of silver and kissed the bride.

Things were bad at that time. When a house could not be got for a married couple, they went straight to the Union House and work was found for both. The Harrisons Hodgsons, Woodwards, Dixons and Morrels, practically kept them from starving before Easingwold Union was built. All of the Mrs. from houses were called Dames; Dame Harrison, Dame Dixon and so on. There were eight thatched cottages for poor people, three were where Mr. Millingon lives and five where John Slater and Mrs. Hall live.

Only violins, flute, clarinet and Bass fiddle were used at Church, and some of the best voices which Husthwaite was noted for.

Wheat was all shorn in those days, and then when barley and oats began to be sown, they began to mow with scythes, and thrashed with flails and the family went out to glean, some families getting as much as three bushels of wheat. Flour being 5s per stone.

I knew several Waterloo veterans. My father was drilled at Thirsk for three months. All the men hired others to go as long as they could, then the married had to go and he went with the first lot. They had to march every day to Sutton to shoot and my mother got food to him, every possible chance there was, they were so badly kept. I knew the Crimean War and all the wars I have known were followed by poverty and want. The manufactories closed down and

---

[1] Mr. Taylor was the great grandfather of the late Maurice 'Doc' Taylor. They both lived at Bank Cottage.

the men came out to sing, 70 together, and stormed the villages for food, but sang beautifully. I remember them singing 'vital spark' in the front gate of the Black Bull and old Mr. Wailes, the Squire, as he was called gave them a big supper.

The coach ran between Edinburgh and London and changed horses at the Wag, Thormanby. My Grandfather went to London. The rule for the head of the house was to make his will before going He went in a coach called the Highflyer, the other being the Wellington.

I remember having a medal pinned on me by Mrs. Woodward of Baxby Manor when Queen Victoria was crowned.

Only two newspapers came into Husthwaite, for Mr. Nelson and Mrs. Slater and they went round the village. Letters were brought in twice a week from Easingwold and it was said anyone who wanted for a good meal and a glass could open a letter and plaster it up again. This is a tale and I can't say it is true. I have looked on five generations of the Wailes, Slaters and Driffield and am eighty seven years of age.

The Orchard Village

Of all the villages in the North Riding few can have had more orchards compared with its size than Husthwaite. From the early part of the twentieth century until the 1950s apples, plums, pears and damsons were "exported" to various towns and cities; mainly by road to the north-east.

Today there is no commercial use from the orchards (apart from the local shop and parish sales). There were at least twenty seven orchards that were harvested in 1911. In 1990 at least nine had been lost altogether and a further ten to a great extent. Only eight remain as they were in 1911. In addition most of the farms in the area had orchards and fortunately most of these are still intact.

It was said that Husthwaite produced the best plums in the area, especially the Victorias, but others were also grown - Damson, Greengage, Cobbler, New Orleans and Belle le Vane (a large deep purple plum). Pears were also a speciality. Conference, William, Hazel and Tindall were among the varieties grown. A wide range of Apples included Bramley, Keswick, Russett, Improved and Old Fashioned Cockpit and Blenheim Orange. The Blenheim Orange was especially sought after for its good keeping qualities and rustic mellow flavour.

Stacks of wooden trays holding the freshly picked fruit waited for collection often on Sundays. Traders from the wholesale markets came with their waggons to barter and buy. Among these were Thomas Gear from Hordern (Co.Durham) and Ned Cummins and E.P.Chambers both from Seaham Harbour. Fruit also went to local markets at Thirsk and at Christmastide there was a brisk trade in berried holly.

Mr. Chambers after visiting the village for many years brought his family to live at Husthwaite in 1935 setting up a market garden business at Ashmount in the High Street. Mr. Chambers died in May 1954 aged seventy three and Mrs. Chambers left Husthwaite to live with her daughter Nancy at Hanover Farm near Easingwold. Nancy had married Chris Thornton from Angram Hall.

The School

Robert Moncaster (c.1797-15/1/1854) was schoolmaster of Husthwaite for thirty eight years. A new school built in 1836 on land given by William Hotham of Highthorne, was supported partly from the charity funds of the parish. A National school was built in 1858 and enlarged in 1890.

Enclosures and Fields

There was no formal Act of Parliament to regulate the enclosure of fields in Husthwaite and this may have taken place informally in the seventeenth century. A schedule with the tithe map drawn up in 1841 by Mr. Harry Scott of Oulston is in the Borthwick Institute, York. It gives the old names of fields that include Batty Garth; Great, Little and Low Marrs; and Low Sharrol Close. Coal Mires is up the lane from Baxby to Carlton. Tenter Close no doubt takes its name from its place in making linen.

Although at this time the township was enclosed there was a substantial amount of roadside waste, in particular on the road to Easingwold and at the junction of the road from the Town Street with Malton Street near the house Beacon Banks. The last named waste was a sizeable square opposite the gate of Beacon Banks. There were also plots of waste on both sides of the Town Street.

Features which may be noted on the plan are three cottages belonging to the Overseers of the Poor at the east end of the Town Street on the north side being the first block of houses but one; two cottages on the triangle of lands in the middle of the road junction at the parish church; a sharp s-bend on the Easingwold road about half way between Acaster Hill and the lane going down to the Red House (the road has long been straightened out); and at the end of the bridle road to Newburgh starting at Beacon Banks and apparently following the top of the escarpment. The village school is shown almost opposite the church on land described as belong to Amaziah Empson. The Town Street is roughly of its present extent but now the houses seem more scattered.

Farms and Houses

The Goulton family whom for many years lived at Highthorne may have come to the township in James I's reign. Richard Goulton BA was licensed to teach in the free Grammar School at "Cuckeswould" in 1619. Christopher Goulton was steward to the manor of Easingwold and Huby from 1677 to 1716. Christopher Goulton on the other hand is probably the man who was a lieutenant in the North York Militia in 1774. On his death in 1815 the Highthorne estate passed to his grandson William Hotham. If the school was the one built in 1836 on land belonging to William Hotham this means that his house Highthorne must have passed to the Empson family in the period 1836-1844 on Mr. Hotham's death and that Amaziah Empson was its owner in 1844. Whether he occupied Highthorne for any period is not known. In 1852-9 N.Thomas Lumley Hodgson, the son of Nathanial Bryan Hodgson of Sand Hutton Hall was the occupier. James Wilson of Liverpool bought the freehold of Highthorne from the Empsons in 1885. In 1923 the owner occupier was Rhodes Hebblethwaite. The pond at Highthorne has been regarded as an old fishpond.

Of the farms shown on Henry Scott's plan of 1841 Baldrence is an old one being mentioned in the parish registers of Easingwold in 1782. The house at Acaster Hill at that date is not the one that stands there now, which was built by Thomas Harrison in 1858. His son William was in occupation in 1890 and in 1923 it was occupied by a Mr. Hugill. Old Mr. Taylor talked of an old thatched house at Acaster Hill, no doubt demolished to make way for the present one.

Red House and Throstle Nest were also thatched houses in the early part of the nineteenth century. It is a little strange that the plan of 1841 does not seem to show Woolpotts since this was built in 1840 by George Potts, a woolmerchant though some of its outbuildings are dated 1846. Mr.Taylor referred to an old thatched house at Woolpotts but this hardly seems so. In the time of the Easingwold Staghounds that is in the 1860's and 1870s, Woolpotts was occupied by the Batty family who were strong supporters of the hunt and the hounds were kept there in pens remaining at least until 1909.

The Beacon

At the highest point of Husthwaite village known as Beacon Banks, near to the Ordnance Survey trigometrical pillar, there once stood a Beacon that may have acted as a signal point during the Roman occupation. At the time of the Spanish Armada in 1588 it was known as "Suncliffe Beacon" and was linked with Whitwell to the south and Ampleforth to the east as part of a continuous beacon chain across the English countryside. On a clear day the view from this point is extensive. To the south and south-west is the Vale of York with the Minster visible, on the north and east the Hambleton Hills and Byland Abbey and to the west and north-west the hills of Wensleydale and the mountains of Craven and Lancashire.

The Beacon was maintained as part of a national system by the inhabitants of Birdforth wapentake and at Thirsk Quarter Sessions on 27th April 1625 it was presented that the Husthwaite Beacon had blown down and it was ordered to be re-erected. Sir Thomas Bellasis and Roger Gregory were to arrange the contract for this.

In 1666 during the Dutch wars signalling by beacons was again practised and again during the Napoleonic wars. Some Yorkshire beacons survived into the nineteenth century. In July 1988 a bonfire, organised by Thirsk Round Table, was lit on the top of Sutton Bank at a ceremony to commemorate the defeat of the Armada as part of a chain of bonfires at strategic points throughout the country.

To the west of the beacon site next to Malton Street is a house built in the middle of last century by the Wailes family known as Beacon Banks and Lists House. William Wailes was a tenant of Lists Field in 1687 and his descendants were to be residents and landowners in the village well into this century. A tombstone to a William Wailes who died in 1796 stands in the church yard. He was Clerk of the Peace for the North Riding and "distinguished for the profession of Law and integrity of mind". In 1880 Francis Wailes (Barrister) lived at Beacon Banks with his wife Emily and son Francis. A Wailes is said to have invented a lawnmower and sold the patents to Ransome. The family last occupied the house in 1950 when Mrs. Majorie Etson Rowe (nee Wailes) moved to Rose Cottage in the village where she died in 1976 at the age of ninety-one years.

The Pubs

In January 1855 the Black Bull was kept by William Taylor. Both the Black Bull and the Smith's or Blacksmith's Arms were open in 1857. William Taylor still had the Black Bull in 1865 when William Cooper was the landlord of the Smith's Arms. In 1890 William Taylor still held the former public house being besides its landlord a shoemaker, a farmer and holding the offices of parish clerk and bailiff of the court leet of the manor. The Black Bull ceased to trade in

The Black Bull pub - now a listed building!

1938 and its landlord Mr. Frank Moncaster moved to the Blacksmiths Arms.

Husthwaite Gate Station

Husthwaite Gate, the first station on the Thirsk to Malton line had the following facilities; one platform, one weighbridge, a weigh office and a waiting room which was added later. The station master's house was set back from the track unlike any other on the T and M route.

In 1880, a timber merchant, Mr. Frank from Helmsley, paid for a tram line to run from Husthwaite Gate to Angram Wood 200 yards away and it is almost certain that this was of narrow gauge and similar to one from Gilling Station to Ampleforth College which was in existence until just before the T and M's closure.

Those Who Served and Stayed On

Rev. George Gill

The **Rev. George Gill** became Vicar of Husthwaite with Carlton and Birdforth on 1898 and stayed on for the long period of thirty three years, retiring in October 1931. He came to live in the Vicarage at Husthwaite with his wife, daughter Ruth and son Claude. The wages of clergy then were very low. The fees for a Burial were 1s 1d and the Clerk's fee 1s, for the publication of Marriage Banns the fee was also 1s 1d, the marriage ceremony fee was 2s 6d - to quote "hours of marriage to take place between 8am and 2pm". It was said that Mr.Gill always identified himself with every good cause for the welfare of the village and district and was an unfailing friend and wise counsellor.

Also giving long service to the church serving under the Rev. Buffey and Rev. Gill was **Mr. Harry Barton** who was verger for thirty seven years. Mrs. Barton also served the church for

The men at Slater's "firm".

circa 1910.

John Robert Slater fourth from left at rear.

thirty years as caretaker. Harry and Annie were married in 1909 and celebrated fifty years of marriage in February 1959. ''Truly good Samaritans'' it was said. For thirty two years Harry worked at Baxby Manor and nine years at Providence Hill Farm.

Miss Grace Taylor

Miss Grace Taylor for fifty years served Husthwaite and Coxwold churches as organist and lived at Bank Cottage in Husthwaite. She had a reputation as a writer of verses. In 1887 she wrote her first poem. She had acknowledgement for poems she wrote by the Royal family; one being on the marriage of the Princess Elizabeth and the Duke of Edinburgh. A poem named ''Golden Wedding Bells'' was accepted by Sir George Wombwell and Lady Julia on their Golden Wedding.

Dr. McKim for forty one years was the doctor in Coxwold and surrounding areas. In Sept 1973 he was presented with a panelled oak corner cupboard made by the local wood carver Wilfred Hutchinson, in gratitude for his service to patients.

Mr. Harold Hutchinson came from Shipton to Alford House, Husthwaite in 1917 where he helped on the farm. He married Jessie Moncaster in 1921 and then moved into the village where he started up a local garage repairing cars and cycles. Later he set up a local bus service and haulage business. He died in December 1976 and his sons Leslie and Geoffrey carried on the business. His other son Wilfred set up as a wood carver in the village; his symbol is a squirrel.

Miss Louie (Ward) Cariss lived in the village for ninety three years. She was known in the village as Louie and lived in the ''Little Cottage'' where in her younger days she would bake teacakes, bread and cakes to sell to the local people for tea. For many years she collected for the Bible Society. She recalled there being six shops in the village at one time during her early life, which included a cobblers shop and a corn and poultry store. She died in March 1988, the last two years spent at Tanpit Lodge in Easingwold away from her little cottage.

The Rev. Goodburn Buffey came to Husthwaite in 1931 and now in 1990 the family stays on. Before coming to the village the Rev. Buffey was vicar of Levisham with Lockton for nearly eight years where it was said ''he earned the love and trust of everyone in the parish''. Mr. and Mrs. Buffey had two sons, Thomas and Clement. Tom

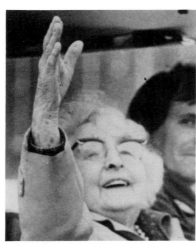

Mrs. Buffey takes to the air at 90.

served in the army during the 1939-45 war years and afterwards became Amenity Officer with the Northumberland River Authority and was a well known lecturer, ornithologist and broadcaster. It was he who arranged for his mother to take her first flight in an aeroplane at the age of ninty, no less, from Teesside Airport. Sadly Tom died in 1989 at the age of sixty five. Clement, the younger son, stays on at Husthwaite living on the farm at Angram Hall. In 1973 he was made people's warden for the parish of Husthwaite with Carlton. Mrs. Buffey celebrated her ninety fifth birthday in November 1989 and is still a regular attender at the village church.

Local Builders

In 1583 a Mr. W. Fox lived in Coxwold and was a stonemason. His descendants later came to live in Husthwaite. Clarence House on The Nooking, Bank Top, was built by them in the 1800s. Members of the family have operated their own building trade for centuries. They have been closely associated with the Newburgh estate (a Mr. Fox is recorded as building the wall around the park) and they have done much work on the local schools and churches. In 1890 Husthwaite had a Brass Band with Mr. Isaac Fox as Bandmaster. Now in the 1990s Isaac's grandson, **Raymond Fox**, with his son Tony continues the family tradition.

The Firm

In or around 1840 John Slater who was born at Oulston set himself up as an agricultural engineer in The Nooking at Husthwaite. The business became known as 'The Firm Yard' or 'Slater's Firm' and in the 1880s it employed three men and five apprentices. John died in 1894 and his son Thomas took over; after Thomas, John Robert ran the firm.

The business grew and consisted of 'The Paint Shop'; a 'Joiner's Shop'; a Wheelwright, a Furnace and an Office. The Office was a small hut set near the Main Street and opposite were the work shops. There were two separate yards; the top one where the construction and building work went on and the lower yard where the construction materials were stored and where the horses where stabled. Carts were used to collect goods from the local station and take the men to their place of work. They covered a wide area and a gang of work people would be sent to carry out jobs as far away as Lincolnshire. Farm buildings, dutch barns, hen houses, farm carts and cart wheels were constructed. Repairs to farm machinery were carried out; to corn binders, seed drills and ploughs.

Young men went to 'Slater's Firm' to learn a trade and around 1912 nineteen men young and old were employed at the yard. Many apprentices had lodgings at the home of John Robert who then lived at Hazeldene in what is known as Low street in Husthwaite.

By 1930 after the 1st World War there was an agricultural depression and the business gradually declined. The business eventually ceased to trade in 1956. Stanley Slater, the son of John Robert and brother to Cynthia and Dorothy, was at the time looking after the firm after John Robert had died in 1964 aged sixty four. The lower half of the yard was taken over by Cynthia's father-in-law, Mr.W.Wentworth of Thormanby. The top half nearest to the main village street is now used by the local building firm E. Fox and Son as a store for building materials.

It was over a century ago when the 'Slater' family came to Husthwaite and now in 1990 they still stay on.

References;

[1] S.R.Eyre, Agric. Hist. Review, in the press.

[2] T.A.M. Bishop, ''Assarting and the Growth of the Open Fields'', Econ. Hist. Rev., 6 (1935-6).

[3] Cowling's Notes. York City Library.

[4] Mrs. Cynthia Wentworth (nee Slater) for information

18
Thornton-on-the-Hill

Jane Rogers

As you travel up Thornton lane today there is little to suggest that you are passing a former manor house of some substance, the site of a deer park and a medieval village. Yet from documentary evidence and aerial photography together with a little field walking it is possible to obtain a reasonable picture of what must have existed around 1500.

The township of Thornton-on-the-Hill is an area of some thousand acres lying within boundaries which remain reasonably well defined today dividing it into two. Thornton Lane runs from north to south - with the major part of the township in the eastern half. Along the western edge traces of a boundary bank are still visible, whilst a small stream with a good bank form the north western edge - the bank continues up to the northern end of Thornton Lane. On the other side this is lost, but there is a mixed hedge. The least obvious section is from there until it reaches the River Kyle, which marks the southern boundary for a short distance, though this has changed its course slightly.

Originally Thornton was a joined township with Baxby, though both had their own manor houses and mills. The earliest reference to them is in 1086 when the Archbishop of York held one carucate and one bovate there. By 1245/5 Roger de Mowbray had let three carucates to John d'Eyvill (or Daiville) at a rent of 3s. a year. Records in 1275 show a Daiville heavily in debt to the Jews and his property at Thornton had been defined as seventy four acres of arable land and three acres of grass. By 1276 he had regained the manor. It is interesting to speculate why he had been in debt. Had he got on the wrong side when joining Simon de Montfort (later killed at the Battle of Evesham) in his

resistance to the king in the Isle of Ely and needed to "square" his account with the Crown? A John D'Eyvill is recorded amongst those who had taken part in this uprising.

Various legal wrangles took place over the years, but by November 1476 when William Vavasour died (leaving amongst other things, three horses and two cloaks, one of which was crimson, and one with black velvet) it was obviously a holding of some importance. It passed through the hands of the Cholmeleys of Brandsby before becoming part of the Newburgh estate in 1608. However, it was not until 1887 that Baxby formally detached from Thornton and was annexed to Husthwaite township for all civil purposes.

The Manor House

The most helpful source for piecing together this medieval puzzle is a map by William Palmer and William Jones dated 1727 which is entitled, "An accurate survey of Thornton Hill. The Estate of the Rt. Honourable Thomas Lord Fauconberg, Baron of Yarm". [1] Together with the map there is the survey material which names the fields, some of the farms and lists the tenants. Altogether there were approximately twenty three tenants but only six farms - it is difficult to give an absolute list of tenants because some of the names have disappeared. The houses shown on the map form the basis of the farms which now exist, though there is no house where Garbutts Ghyll is today. There is an additional farm house - Reynards - which appears on both the 1727 and the 1841 tithe maps and which no longer exists.

We know from William Vavasour's will [2] already quoted that he was a man of substance, presumably with a suitable house of quality. His

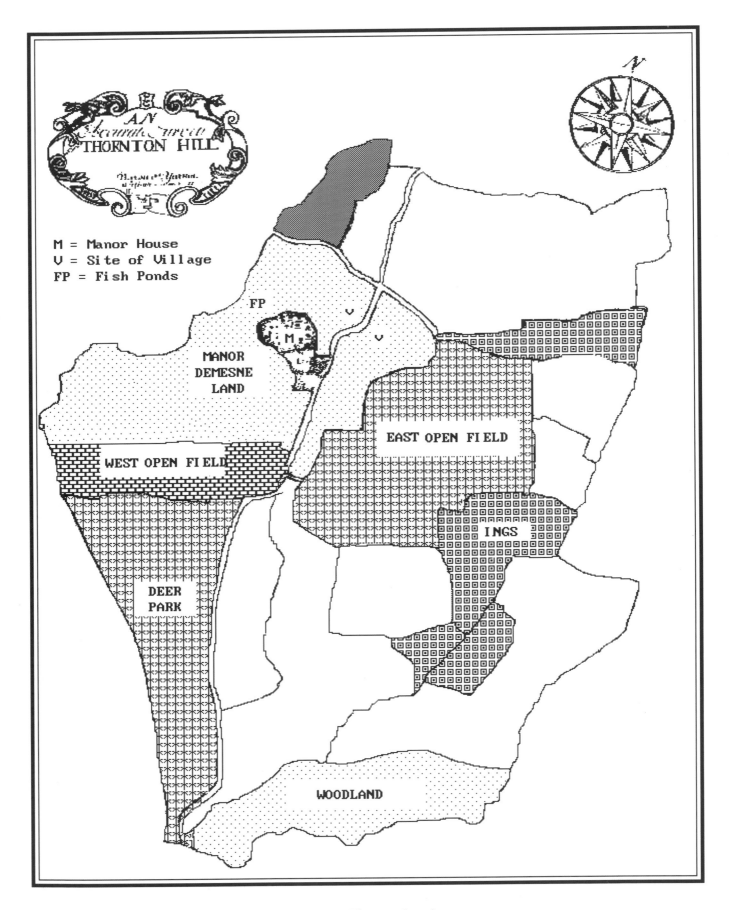

Fifteenth Century Thornton based on

Estate Survey Map 1727 [1]

wife, Elizabeth (of the Daiville family) who is buried at Coxwold, left a will dated 13th June 1498 which endorses this. She left her chaplain, if he was still with her, the sum of six marks per annum if he did not immediately enter chantry. 3s. 4d. was left to Husthwaite church, a vestment and the altar cloths from her private chapel went to the chapel at Oulston and a silver chalice with two candlesticks to Coxwold church to stand on her sepulchre.

This would indicate a wealthy background with a house to match, yet by 1619, a hundred and twenty years later we are told "Thornton is almost desolate now". This is borne out by a description given by Richard Cholmeley of Brandsby in his notebook of a visit he made on 4th October 1616. [3]

"Memorandum that I Richard Cholmeley of Brandsby in the Countye of York esquire made entrye in the manor house of Thornton super monte and was in the parlor in the tenancye

Ridge and Furrow in snow at Thornton-on-the-Hill

occupation of John Horneby as alsoe in an uthouse in the tenancye of one [blank] Skelton in the name of all the lands as well as without the parke pale as with in which were the lands of my late grandfather Sir Richard Cholmeley of Roxeby Knighte whose heire at the common lawe I am. My entry made as a foresaid in the prescens of the said Hornebye's wife, Ould Skelton who kept his bed and done longe of payne in a sore eye and in his bones all on that syde, and his wife, a woman in an other house on the north syde of the court a dweller there, and of my tow men Ambrose Storye and John Sampson".

So between 1500 and 1616 the Manor was still standing with possibly a courtyard and certainly

other dwellings. It is difficult to classify an "uthouse". But the entry is certainly a description of a run down property - not a thriving manor. This is born out when two years later we are told "Thornton is desolate now". In 1680 the Newburgh accounts record "staying and propping the house at Thornton".

Where was this Manor House? The Survey map is called an accurate survey and we have no call to doubt it. It is therefore interesting to note that each of the carefully drawn farmhouses is different, so it must be reasonable to assume that even if only a fair representation stood on the site it could be an indication of comparable sizes. In addition the Hearth Tax records of both 1662 [5] and 1672 [6] only record one house with two hearths. So, as there is only one house shown with two chimneys - which is also quite a bit larger than any of the others, might this not be the Manor? Another helpful indication is that the closes immediately opposite are called dovecote garth and dovecote hill, though no buildings remain. Dovecotes were a manorial feature.

The house on the map is two storied with the chimneys at either end. There is a large central main door with windows either side, both upstairs and down, with two more windows, upstairs and down on the western end. Near the entrance gate from Thornton Lane is what could be a stable block with no windows but a very wide door. It is a tall building with a small single storied out shoot. At the rear of this are further buildings in an inverted "L" shape. The large bit has no chimney nor window, but the "arm" is a single storied building with an upper door. This is possibly a block of barns, with the entrance on

1. Tenant to reside, pay taxes, build a fold yard adjoining house if desired and keep all fences, gates, styles etc. in repair.

2. Tenant has to drain with stone in an effective manner all such parts of the farm as require it so that the whole shall be completed by 1804.

3. To be allowed to plough land as he wanted as set out by the Agent taking no more than 2 crops to a fallow and laying down to grass the second fallow well cleared and tilled with 3 cauldrons of lime to an acre then sown with seed of cow grass, white clover and hay but not rye grass, to till the plough lands with lime and lay all the manure and compost on the meadow except such part that they may need for raising a few turnips or potatoes

4. To scour out all the fences and ditches annually.

5. Not to top dress any pollards or timbers but to nurse all trees likely to become such, to weed and dress all newly planted fences twice a year for three years.

6. Not to sow any arable land with rape for seed or with teazles, weld, hemp, flax or mustard.

7. Not to have more stock in the last year of the lease than in earlier years.

8. To pay 3s. an acre for grass land ploughed with consent and £10 without licence. Land improperly laid to grass to be ploughed out and sown with peas and beans then fallowed and tilled with three cauldrons of lime per acre and then sown with oars and grass seed.

9. Waygoing crops to be thrashed on the premises leaving the straw on the farm - paying 20s an acre for standage and 4s. an acre for tythe.

10. Tenants to have rough timber for repairs and to get stone to burn lime or for draining in places assigned. Incoming tenants to enter after 1st January to dress meadow ground and pasture and to plough and sow all arable. Not plant winter corn.

11. Tenants shall agree to give up land or make exchanges and give or accept more land at any time in the first year of the term.

12. Lessors reserves quarries, all timber and other wood.

13 Lessees to ensure all hay and straw to be consumed on premises. There is a separate contract for tythe.

Newburgh Farm Lease 1796

the other side. In addition a short distance away from these buildings are two single storied houses joined at right angles to one another - each with a very small amount of ground, probably only a few feet, to the front. There is a boundary round all the buildings and a small orchard which encompasses about two acres - eight acres in all when the adjoining orchard is included. I wonder whether the small "L" shaped houses on the map are the remains of the courtyard.

The present house on this site is High House Farm in the northwest section of the township. Though now bearing little resemblance externally to the large house on the map it has interesting features. There is a large externally stepped chimney stack - indicating an inglenook type of fireplace inside. Beside it is a small single lancet "window" with a flat arched head - both are indicators of an earlier building.

Further evidence is provided by aerial photographs which show the remnants of fishponds to the north of the house (essential to provide part of the inhabitants diet). It is interesting to note that the present owners of High House have alder trees on the site as little else will thrive in such boggy ground.

The Deer Park

Richard Cholmeley's entry refers to lands within and without the "parke pale", and the 1577 Saxton Map of Yorkshire shows a Park at Thornton. This implied major capital expenditure on someone's part as there had to be very high banks dug out with the ditch on one side and twelve foot high palings made of split oak on the top. It is shown on the Speed Map of 1627 but does not appear on the Survey Map of 1723. In the Quarter Session Records of 1618 there is a mention of the highway lying "juxta pallias de Thornton" (against the pales of Thornton). The highway referred to is described as that between the village of Husthwaite and How Hill - Thornton Lane leading to Easingwold.

When walking the Thornton boundaries the remnants of the Park bank can be seen on the western edge. This would seem to place the park in the south western quarter of the township. The circumference of the long narrow section between there, the top of the hill and Thornton Lane is precisely two miles. A muster roll of 1569 reported a park at Thornton, which had two mares - one bay, one grey and a compass of two miles. There seems little doubt therefore where the deer park lay. As the Manor declined in importance from 1500 onwards it was presumably made during the long ownership of the Daivilles.

We can now place the manor and the deer park on the map - what about the village?

The Village and Villagers

A deed of 1486 refers to four houses which fronted onto the high road and had the East Common Field of Thornton behind them - presumably, therefore, facing west. Aerial photographs suggest there may have been buildings to the north of the manor. In 1608 when the manor was conveyed to the Newburgh Estate it contained twenty cottages and twenty messuages - few of which are visible on the 1727 map, though twenty three tenants were listed then. What did show up were six dwellings approximately where today's farm houses are.

Glimpses of these cottages and tenants appear in various records. For example, "Ould Skelton"'s wife referred to in Richard Cholmeley's visit to the manor house died a year later to the day according to the Church records him dying a couple of months later in December His daughter married seventeen years before. John Hornbie had married in 1589 and lived to 1638. [7] He had seven children - two of whom were girls, who married in their early twenties outside the immediate neighbourhood. One name "Bayllye" or Bailey is an archer with horses and harness on the muster roll in 1539. The same name is on the subsidy list for 1544, the muster roll of 1613, the tenant's list in 1609 and the Hearth Tax of 1672, possibly all from the same family. Six tenant familes held the same land in 1609 and 1720 and one - the Barkers were still there at the time of the 1851 census. Between 1610 to 1620 only seven different family names are recorded for Thornton - including a Raper at Wank Mill. Rapers are still farming on the hill, though not the same family. In the early 18th century tenants had their fines as recusants paid for by their landlord. Perhaps it helped to be a Roman Catholic if one required a tenancy on the Newburgh estate

Fields and Woodland

Most of the inhabitants of Thornton worked on the land - with a few employed as house servants on the farms. Many of the fields they worked in bore their own names - Coupland, Cundall, Snowden, Thompson, Tiplady, Pears, Barker, all appear both as close names and as tenants in 1679 as well as being in the church records at the beginning of the century. It is possible that they were living nearby whilst still retaining their Thornton links..

Today the fields are often referred to by size, e.g. Ten Acres, or position, Top Field. However, all the hills are still known by the 1727 names, Elmer Hill, Barker Hill and Round Hill. Previously the closes were named by use - Great Horse and Little Horse Closes, Calf Close, Corn Close and Winter close. There was also a priest close which probably had some connection with the priest at Oulston as it was on the boundary with that village (and some tenants held land in both villages and also in Husthwaite). Toad Mires is on the spring line and Vinion (venison?)

101

in the deer park area. Stony Flatts, Long Strip Close, Haggs, Ings and Pastures also indicate the type of usage - as do Orchard Bank and Dovecote Garth.

The earliest reference we have to named fields is 7th January 1414 when a deed refers to the common land of Thornton and names fields called Short Kirkgate and Broadends. A later deed of 24th December 1486 refers to East Common Field which implies more than one common field. The earlier deed (1414) gave the Prior and convent of Newburgh leave to enclose Short Kirkgates with a ditch and hedges and hold it separately from the rest of the common field. The later deed (1486) refers to five closes; Eastfield, Peron Close, Chamber Close. le Bewstacegarth and the Lady Close. Enclosure in this manor was therefore taking place as early as the fifteenth century though there was never a formal enclosure Act.

Incidently one of the names on the Survey map is Brewster Close - lying south of the track from Oulston to Husthwaite. Aerial photographs and site walking now prove conclusively that this was an area of ridge and furrow - surely Eastfield. It was probably divided into two as the field edges would seem to indicate that the ridge and furrow pattern went from north to south in one half and from east to west in the other. A water course runs through the two sections which has irregular shaped fields following it named as "ings" and "pasture". In fact some of them remain as grazing land today.

So we can imagine where early lords of the manor hunted - where tenants worked on the fields, their pasture land lay and their animals were kept. Fish came from the ponds and doves from the dovecotes. What about wood for fuel, housing or fencing? Another look at the Survey Map shows a heavily wooded area of approximately fifteen acres a quarter of a mile off Thornton Lane to the east, just north of the original wooded section of the township. The field shape remains on the tithe map and even today it is unaltered. It would be interesting to known why so much woodland had remained in this particular area, whilst it had virtually disappeared elsewhere, just leaving the close names ending in "hagg", indicating previous woodland.

So by careful examination of various maps and the use of existing records - we are lucky in having good estate accounts over a long spell - it is possible to piece together a little of the life of a small community over nearly 500 years. The 1723 map was the starting point - the finishing one will be the farm lease of 1796.

Sources

[1] "An Accurate Survey Map for Lord Fauconberg. 1727". NYCRO. ZDV V1 6: MIC 1504/390405.

[2] Will of William Vavasour. Cowling's Notes.

[3] Richard Cholmondely Notebook. NYCRO.

[4] Newburgh Estate Papers. NYCRO.

[3] Tithe Map 1841. Borthwick Institute.

[5] PRO. E179 315/452. 1662.

[6] PRO E179 261/32 1672.

[7] Parish Records. NYCRO.
Thornton on the Hill Manor Land (1260 - 1609) NYCRO. MIC 1352.

[8] Muster Rolls. PRO. Subsidy List PRO., E179 211/100.

Index

A

Agriculture **44-49**

    Bellasis 48

    Black Death 44

    Bovates 10, 13

    Butter Trade 48

    Carlton Open Fields 10

    Carucates 10, 12, 13

    Cattle 47

    Climate 44

    Common Land 48, 49

    Dissolution of Monasteries 44

    Field Names 46, 48

    Flax 47

    Hemp 46, 47

    Husthwaite Open Fields 11

    Napoleonic Wars 46

    New Agriculture 46

    Open Fields 46

    Oxen 47

    Population 44

    Reversed S 10

    Sheep 48, 49

    Soils 5

    See Byland and Newburgh Granges

    See Markets

Ampleforth 1, 6, 7, 45

Angram 1, 48, 70, 92, 94, 96

Archbishop of York 6, 8, 10, 12, 25, 91, 97

B

Bagby 20

Balk 20, 22, 23

Battles

    Battle of Byland 21

    Battle of the Standard 15, 19

Baxby 1, 6, 7, 12, 13, 17, 29, 45, 46, **68-73,** 78, 88, 89, 92, 95

    Baxby Mill 22

Baxby Manor 68-70

    Asquith Family 71

    Baxby Family 69, 70

    Chambers Family 70, 71, 73

    Earls of Northumberland 68

    Frank Family 73

    George Denham 71

    Goulton Family 70

    Kitchingham Family 70, 71

    Ragget Family 70

    Skonoker 70

    Thornton Family 71

Baxby Manor House 68, **71-73**

    Base cruck 72

    Oratory 73

Baxby Mill 69, 71

Beacon Banks 92, 93

    Lists House 94

    See World War Two

Bellasis Family 17, 77~79, **83-84**

    Anthony Bellasis 83

    Billingham on Tees 83

    Charlotte 30

    Charlotte Lamb 86

    Charlotte Wynn Belassis 86

    See Civil War

    Family Tree 84

    John, Lord Worlaby 27, 28, 85

    Richard Bellasis 83, 85

    Sir Henry Bellasis 78

    Sir William 78

    Thomas, 1st Visc. Fauconberg 79

    Thomas, 2nd Visc. Fauconberg 85

    Thomas, 4th Visc. Fauconberg 83, 85, 87

    Henry 5th Visc.Fauconberg 86

    See Civil War

Birdforth 1, 3, **74-76,** 78, 91, 93, 94

    Coal Mining 75

    John Horner 75

    Lord Downe 76

    Luke Plummer 76

    Luke Punshon 76

    Mrs. Thornton 75

    St. Mary's Church 74

Birdforth Wapentake 7, 27, 74, 93

    Burtree House 74

Borthwick Institute 92

Boscar 22, 63

Byland 1

Byland Abbey 15, 17, **18-23,** 69, 71

    Angram Grange 22, 23

    Charters 22

    Cistercian Order 18

    Clairvaux Abbey 18

    Drainage 20

    Fish Ponds 20, 24

    Furness Abbey 18

    Gunreda 19

Hood 19

Lay Brothers 21

Nidderdale 20

Rievaulx Abbey 19, 22, 25, 26

Roger de Mowbray 19

Savignac Order 20

Sheep 22

Sir William Pickering 19, 22, 23

Stocking 22

Thorpe 22

Wildon 22

C

Cambe 22, 48

Carlton Husthwaite 1, 3, 6, 7, 10, 12, 13, 45, 46, 58, 60, 74, 76

    Kytchinghams 46

Civil War **27-29**, 56

    Captain Alan Baines 28

    Commonwealth 28

    Farnley Wood Plot 28

    George Denham 28, 71

    John Bellasis 27, 28

    Local Inhabitants 28

    Lord Wharton of Byland 27

    Mary Cromwell 28

    Militia 27, 29

    Restoration 29

    Sir Henry Slingsby 27, 28

    Sir Walter Vavasour 27, 28

    Thomas, 1st Visc. Fauconberg 27

    See Quakers

Coxwold 1, 3, 5, 6, 17, 29, 45, 48, 49, 74, 75, **77-81**, 86

    Almshouses 80

    Annual Fair 77

    Colville Hall 17, 78

    Coxwold Station 81

    Earls of Northumbria 78

    Estate Centre 78

    Fauconberg Arms 80

    Free Grammar School 79

    Pottery 77

    Prison House 80

    Shandy Hall 79

Sidney Sussex College 80

Sir John Harte 79

Thirsk and Malton Railway 81

Wombwell Family 77

See Bellasis Family

See Domesday Survey

Coxwold Church 78, 89, 99

    Bellasis Monuments 78

    Breeches Bible 79

Coxwoldshire 1, 45~49, 78, 81

Craftsmen

    Charles Mitley 86

    Cortese 86

    Daniel Harvey 86

    Edward Mortimer 86

    Fox Family 79

    Robert Thompson 90

Crayke 29

D

Domesday Survey 1, 6, 8, 45, 68, 74, 78

E

Early Settlers

    Mesolithic 5

    Neolithic 5

Easingwold 62~64, 66, 67, 93

Easingwold Advertiser 52

Easingwold Staghounds 93

Easingwold Union 91

Education **30-36**

    1870 Education Act 32

    Attendance 35

    Board Schools 32

    Church Schools 31

    Inspectors 31, 33~35

    Lady Payne-Gallwey 31, 35

    Log Books 31, 33, 35, 36

    National Schools 31, 36

    Newcastle Commission 31

    Scholarships 36

    School Boards 32~36

    Sunday Schools 30, 31

    See Schools

Enclosures 45

F

Farms

    Acaster Hill 12, 62, 91, 93

    Baldrence 93

    Flower o' May 62, 88

    Garbutts Ghyll 97

    Hanover Farm 92

    High House Farm 100

    Lodge Farm 62

    Red House 91, 93

    Reynards 97

    Sand Hill 13

    Sandhill Farm 62

    Sunley Farm 56, 62

    Throstle Nest 22, 71, 89, 91, 93

    Woolpots 12, 29, 71, 91, 93

Field Names 92, 101

G

Galtres Forest 12, 78, 88

Geology 1

    Coxwold-Gilling Gap 74, 77

    Hambleton Hills 1, 3

    Howardian Hills 3, 88

    Ice Age 3

    Jurassic 1

    Jurassic Coal 75

    Kimmeridge Clay 3

    Lake Pickering 3

    Vale of Pickering 3

    Vale of York 3

Gerlestre

    See Birdforth Wapentake

H

Hearth Tax Returns 99, 101

Highthorne 12, 91~93

    Cameron 88

    Empson 93

    Fishpond 93

    Goulton 90, 93

    Hebblethwaite 93

    Hodgson 93

    Hotham 92

Wilson 91
See World War Two
Hovingham 20
Husthwaite 3, 12, 29, 45~48, 68~71, **88-96**
Bank Cottage 91
Barton Harry 94
Buffey Family 95
Cowling's Notes 96
Domesday 88, 89
Dr. McKim 95
Enclosures 92
Field Names 92
Gibbet Corner 91
Highthorne 88
Husthwaite Church 24
Husthwaite School 92
Hutchinson Harold 95
Louie (Ward) Cariss 95
Methodism 91
Mr. Taylor's Account 91
New Village 88
Open Fields 88
Orchards 92
Overseers of the Poor 93
Prebendary 89
Raymond Fox 96
Roman Coins 88
Slater John Robert 96
Suncliffe 48
Taylor Grace 95
The Firm 96
The Nooking 61, 96
Tithe Map 88, 92
Wentworth Family 96
See Beacon Banks
See Education
See Malton Street
See Ulfr
See World War Two
Husthwaite Beacon 93
Dutch Wars 93
Suncliffe Beacon 93
Thirsk Quarter Sessions 93

Husthwaite Church
Ecclesiastical Commissioners 91
Hagioscope 90
Norman Architecture 89
St. Nicholas' 88, 89
Trinity College 89, 91
Hutton Sessay 8

K
Kilburn 1, 6, 8, 17, 24, 68, 69, 76, 78~80

L
Local Residents 16th Cent.
Alan Storey 48
Local Residents 17th Century
George Wailes 48
John Myers 71
Mr. Kay 48
Local Residents 19th Century
Batty 93
Cooper 94
Dixon 91
Hall 91
Harrison
Hodgson 91
Millington 91
Morrel 91
Potts 93
Rudd 91
Sheperd 91
Slater 91
Taylor 91, 94
Tesseyman 91
Warin 91
Woodward 91
Wragg 91
Yallow 91
Local Residents 20th Century
Chambers 92
Edwards 94
Etson Rowe 94
Harrison 89
Hugill 93
Taylor 91
Thornton 92

M
Markets
Coxwold 77
Northallerton 47
Thirsk 48
York 48
Metcalfe's Diary 76
Mowbray Family **14-16**, 97
Ann 14
Battle of Hitten 15
Gunreda 15
Honour of Mowbray 15, 16, 68
John, Lord Mowbray 16
Matilda 14
Nigel d'Aubigny 14, 16
Roger de 1, 15, 69, 78
Roger de Montbray 14
Thomas 1st Duke of Norfolk 16
Vale of Mowbray 14
William de Mowbray 24
William Mowbray 15
Muster Roll 101

N
Newburgh 1, 28, 61, 75, **82-87**
Deer Park 86
Garden
Oliver Cromwell 82
Park 87
Pleasure Garden 87
Stephen Switzer 87
The Mount 87
The Stripe 87
See Bellasis Family
See Craftsmen
See Wombwell Family
Newburgh Estate 46, 49, 101
Farm Lease 100
Newburgh Priory 1, 15, 17, **23-27**, 24, 78, 82, 89
Augustinian Canons 24
Boundaries 82
Brian 12, 24
Bridlington Priory 24
Brink 25

Dissolution
  Granges 25
  Hood 25
  Margaret Tudor 25
  Roger de Mowbray 24
  Thorpe 25
  William de Newburgh 82
  Yearsley 25
Norman Conquest 6
  Arnketil 6, 8
  Battle of Tinchebrai 14
  Cofsi 1, 6, 7, 14, 78
  Gospatric 7
  Harrying of the North 8, 45, 78
  Hugh Son of Baldric 6, 8, 14, 45, 78
  Morcar 7
  Robert de Stuteville 15
  Robert (Earl of Northumbria) 14, 17
  Robert of Normandy 14
  Tostig 7, 14
Norman Families
  Cholmeley 97, 101
  Colville 17, 78
  Daiville 17, 20, 22, 68, 69, 71, 97
  de Stuteville 14, 15
  Malbisse 16
  Maunsell 16
  Meynill 19, 23
  Nevill 23
North York Militia 93

O

Old Byland 22
Oldstead 3
Osgodby 6, 22, 45
Oulston 1, 3, 5, 7, 10, 12, 17, 25, 78, 92, 97, 101, 102
Over Stilton 78

P

Parish Magazines 50
Peckitt William **40-43**
  Biagio Rebecca 43
  Coats of Arms 43

Cumberland Row, York 43
Dr. John Wall 43
Family Tree
Glass Painting 40
Henry Gyles 42
Husthwaite 40
Louis XIII 42
Mary Mitley 40
New College Oxford 43
Peckitt Street, York 43
St Martin cum Gregory 43
York Guildhall 40
Pilgrimage of Grace 23
Population 8
Pubs
  Black Bull 92, 94
  Blacksmiths Arms 94
  Fauconberg Arms 80

Q

Quakers
  Isaac Lindley 29
  Local Quakers 29
  See Civil War

R

Rievaulx 19
Rivers and Streams
  Elphin Beck 3, 88
  Holbeck 20
  Long Beck 24
  River Foss 88
  River Kyle 88, 97
  River Swale 75, 88
Roads
  A19 74, 75
  Drove Road 82
  Malton Street 5, 88, 92, 94
  Royal Routes 75

S

Schoolmasters 33
  Arthur Mortimer 33
  George Meyrick 32
  George Whitfield 35
  James Duck 33

Matthew Sowerby 34, 35, 74
Rev. T. Midgely 90
Richard Goulton 93
Robert Dawson 31
Rev. Thomas Newton 80
Robert Moncaster 30, 92
William Nelson 31
Schools
  Birdforth 31~36
  Carlton Husthwaite 30, 32, 35, 36
  Coxwold 30~32, 35, 36
  Coxwold Free Grammar School 30
  Easingwold 36
  Free Grammar School 79
  Husthwaite 30, 31
  Oulston 30
  Thirkleby 31~33, 35, 36
  Yearsley 30
  See World War Two
Sterne Laurence **37-39**, 77, 79~81
  Archbishop Sterne 37
  A Sentimental Journey 39, 77
  Burials 39
  Dean Fountayne 38
  Elizabeth Lumley 37, 39
  Eliza Draper 38
  Hipperholme School 37
  Jacques Sterne 37
  Kitty Fourmantel 38
  Laurence Sterne Trust 39
  London 38
  Lydia Sterne 37~39
  Minster Yard 39
  Shandy Hall 38, 79
  Tristram Shandy 37, 77
  Tuberculosis 37
  Vicar of Coxwold 37
  Vicar of Stillington 38
  Vicar of Sutton-on-Forest 37
Suncliffe 56

T

Thirkleby 1, 3, 6, 23, 24, 29, 45, 46, 48, 49, 78

See World War Two

Thirsk 15, 16

Thirsk to Malton Railway 81, 88, 91, 94

    Husthwaite Gate Station 94

Thomas Cromwell 83

Thormanby 8, 92, 96

Thornton-on-the-Hill 1, 3, 6, 8, 17, 45, 68~71, **97-102**

    Baxby 97

    Cholmely 99, 101

    Daiville 97, 99, 101

    Deer Park 97, 101

    Field Names 101

    Garbutts Ghyll 97

    Manor House 97, 99, 101

    Medieval Village 97, 101

    Robert de Mowbray 97

    Roger de Mowbray 97

    Saxton Map 101

    Speed Map 101

    Survey Map 98

    The Villagers 101

    William Vavasour 97

    Woodland 102

Thorpe 7, 10, 20, 22, 23, 25

Tithe 46

Tithe Survey 13

Trinity College 45, 70

U

Ulfr 1, 6, 12, 13, 14, 68, 75

    Ulfr's Horn 8

V

Vicars

    George Gill 74, 94

    Goodburn Buffey 95

    H.G.Tyler 91

    John Winter 90

    Rev. George Gill 52

    Robert Peirson 90

    T.Midgely 90

Victoria Cottage **54-60**

    Appleby Family 58

Calvert Family 55

Driffield Family 60

Gamble Family 55

Hobkyn Family 55

Newby Hall 58

Nicholson Family 60

Robinson Family 54

Sharrow Family 55

Weddell Family 54

W

Wailes Family 52, 90, 92, 94

Wapentake 76

Wildon 22, 23, 29, 48

Wildon Grange 6, 8, 13

Wombwell Family 77, **86-87**

    Beryl Tilley 86

    Capt. V.M.Menzies 64, 81, 83, 86, 87

    Charge of Light Brigade 86

    Julia Wombwell 86

    Sir George 3rd Bt. 86

    Sir George Orby 4th Bt. 77, 78, 86

    Sir George 7th Bt.83, 87

    Woodland 45

World War Two **61-67**

    231st Field Company 62

    146th Field Ambulance Co. 62

    30th Armoured Brigade 62

    69th Field Regiment 62

    17th Platoon D Company 64

    4th Lincolns 62

    Airfields 63

    Beacon Banks 63~65, 67

    Bert Kingsley 62

    Dora Bragg 67

    Easingwold 61

    Evacuees 61

    Flax Factory 65, 66

    Freddie Richmond 62

    Hallamshire Battalion 62

    Highthorne 62, 65, 67

    Home Gaurd 64, 65

    Husthwaite School 61

    Husthwaite W.I. 66

Land Army 67

London Rifles 62

Malton Street 62

Miss C. Callaway 66

Mr. D.M. Francis 61

Pig Club 67

Roll of Honour 67

Searchlight Station 61~64

St. Richards School 62

Thirkleby Prisoner Camp 66

Winter Sports 61

York and Lancaster Regiment 62

Y

Yearsley 1, 5, 6, 8, 17, 20, 22, 23, 25, 28, 49, 75, 78

York Minster 8, 45